THE LIBRARY OF HOLOCAUST TESTIMONIES

Good Beyond Evil

Good Beyond Evil

EVA GOSSMAN

VALLENTINE MITCHELL
LONDON • PORTLAND, OR

First published in 2002 in Great Britain by
VALLENTINE MITCHELL
Crown House, 47 Chase Side, Southgate
London N14 5BP

and in the United States of America by
VALLENTINE MITCHELL
c/o ISBS, 5824 N.E. Hassalo Street
Portland, Oregon, 97213-3644

Website: www.vmbooks.com

British Library Cataloguing in Publication Data
Gossman, Eva
  Good beyond evil. – (The library of Holocaust testimonies)
  1. Gossman, Eva – Childhood and youth. 2. Reinitz (Family)
  3. Jewish women – Biography 4. World War, 1939–1945 – Jews –
  Rescue – Slovakia 5. Righteous Gentiles in the Holocaust –
  Slovakia
  I. Title
  940.5'318'092

ISBN 0-85303-446-X (paper)
ISSN 1363-3759

Library of Congress Cataloging-in-Publication Data

A catalog record for this book is available
from the Library of Congress

Gossman, Eva
  Good beyond evil / Eva Gossman.
    p. cm. – (Library of Holocaust testimonies, ISSN 1363-3759)
  ISBN 0-85303-466-X (pbk.)
  1. Holocaust, Jewish (1939–1945)–Personal narratives. 2. Righteous Gentiles
  in the Holocaust–Biography. I. Title. II. Series.

D804.195 .G57 2002
940.53'1835'0922–dc21

2002026516

Typeset in 11/12.25 Palatino by Frank Cass Publishers Ltd
Printed in Great Britain by MPG Books Ltd, Victoria Square, Bodmin, Cornwall

Contents

In Memory of
Mária Göblová Krescanková
(2.1.1915–4.12.1982)

'But the path of the just is as the shining light,
that shineth more and more unto the perfect day.'

(Proverbs, 4:18)

'Give me but one firm spot on which to stand and
I will move the earth.'

(Archimedes)

'And we forget because we must and not because
we will.'

(Matthew Arnold)

List of Illustrations

Between pp.50 and 51

1. Mária Krescanková, before her marriage, age 31 (1946).

2. Šalomon Reinitz, age 40 (1941).

3. Rachel Reinitz, age 36 (1943).

4. Eva Reinitz, age 9; Gabriela Reinitz, age 4; Alexander Reinitz, age 11 (1940).

5. Front: Aunt Rozsi and Uncle Kive Kornitzer. Rear, left to right: Alexander Reinitz; Aunt Ansci Reinitz; Alice, Ocsi and Marica Kornitzer; Eva Reinitz (1943 or 1944).

6. Schoolfriends Nuša and Eva (1948).

7. Eva and Eva (1948).

8. Mária Göblová Krescanková (1960s).

9. Robert Göblov and Mária Göblová Krescanková at the time of their marriage (1953).

10. Mária Göblová Krescanková; Robert Göblov; Vlasta Krescanková (1960s).

11. Vlasta Krescanková receiving Certificate of Honour, Yad Vashem, 3 July 1997.

Acknowledgements

I am grateful to many friends whose love and understanding never wavered, even when I could not bring myself to share drafts of the manuscript with them. They helped immensely in ways that are as real as they are hard to specify.

Two of my close friends, Carol Thompson and Angelica Rudenstine, read the first draft of the manuscript lovingly and critically. They would not let me give up even when I was tempted to do so. A somewhat more polished version was read by my good friend and devoted neighbour, Gisella Berry.

Three editors of scholarly presses, Walter Lippincott, Carole LeFaivre and Joanna Hitchcock gave me valuable advice. Though they cautioned me about the difficult road ahead, they expressed confidence in the manuscript and urged me to persevere.

At Frank Cass, I was fortunate to have Sarah Clarke guide the manuscript through the initial stages of review. I would especially like to thank Georgina Clark-Mazo for her extraordinary attentiveness and excellent advice in the later stages of the editing process.

My brother, Alexander Ben Ami, and my sister, Gabriela Weiss, jogged my memory about half-forgotten places and events. They share responsibility for factual errors.

My daughter Janice was the leader of my cheering section. Her interest, enthusiasm and curiosity kept me going. Her presence at the ceremony at Yad Vashem strengthened my resolve to write the book.

I am especially grateful to my husband, Lionel, who accompanied me on the difficult journey to Slovakia. He made me see greys and flickers of white, when black was all I could see. During the final preparation of the manuscript, he helped with great generosity and good humour.

The Library of Holocaust Testimonies

It is greatly to the credit of Frank Cass that this series of survivors' testimonies is being published in Britain. The need for such a series has been long apparent, where many survivors made their homes.

Since the end of the war in 1945, the terrible events of the Nazi destruction of European Jewry have cast a pall over our time. Six million Jews were murdered within a short period; the few survivors have had to carry in their memories whatever remains of the knowledge of Jewish life in more than a dozen countries, in several thousand towns, in tens of thousands of villages, and in innumerable families. The precious gift of recollection has been the sole memorial for millions of people whose lives were suddenly and brutally cut off.

For many years, individual survivors have published their testimonies. But many more have been reluctant to do so, often because they could not believe that they would find a publisher for their efforts.

In my own work over the past two decades I have been approached by many survivors who had set down their memories in writing, but who did not know how to have them published. I also realized, as I read many dozens of such accounts, how important each account was, in its own way, in recounting aspects of the story that had not been told before, and adding to our understanding of the wide range of human suffering, struggle and aspiration.

With so many people and so many places involved, including many hundreds of camps, it was inevitable that the historians and students of the Holocaust should find it difficult at times to grasp the scale and range of events. The publication of memoirs is therefore an indispensable part of the extension of knowledge, and of public awareness of the crimes that had been committed against a whole people.

Sir Martin Gilbert
Merton College, Oxford

Foreword

Is it all my life I have wanted to go to Slovakia? It feels like it. It is probably better not to go. Better to keep these places in one's head. What does familiarity do? It ruins one's dreams. Tourism is as incompatible with dreams as it is with culture.

Besides: the towns of Slovakia are full of ghosts. I only know the haunted towns of Poland. Once I saw Kafka coming out of a synagogue on Lubartowska Street in Lublin. Or was that only in a photograph? Or was it someone else?

At a Catholic funeral on Lipowa Street in that black magical city, I was sure it was the Emperor Maximilian that I saw in his coffin on a day of Mexican heat. It was not. It was the body of my dear friend, Andrzej Nowodworski. He was as good a friend of Jews as Mária Krescanková had been.

I am reminded of the artist Shimon Attie and his slide projections onto the walls of Jewish Berlin: ghostly visions of the dead among the living.

The lively dead: how do we project them? Onto the walls we know. That wall in the Lublin ghetto my son photographed: I see Kitty Hart running past it with a letter to post or with a book of English grammar to deep death from the door. Or the sewer covers of the Old Town in Warsaw: stumbling over them, do you remember the boys and girls of April 1943 and August 1944? As I do.

I projected Janko M. onto the walls of Presov. He is seated under the rowan trees eating a green peach. But now it is Teta whom I project. She is sitting at her desk at the entrance to the *mikva*. She is eating a cucumber while watching Eva at play in the courtyard of the Jewish community building.

I invented Janko M., but Mária K. there is no need to invent. Fact is better than fiction. I should explain: why I am writing like this.

Many years ago I wrote a story. It was written in response to a competition in a Catholic weekly paper. We were asked to write about saints, or about novelists, or about both: I have forgotten which. Possibly the challenge was in the title I gave my story: 'Can a Novelist be a Saint?' My saintly novelist was an invention.

He was born on a farm near Bardejov in 1902. He became a clerk in government service and was promoted to head of department at Presov in 1938. His only novel was published in 1932; it was called *The Easter Incident* and was well received by the intellectual set in Bratislava. He did all he could to help Jews persecuted by the Tiso regime. In 1944 he sewed a Star of David onto the breast pocket of his best suit and with false papers joined the last group of Jews deported to Auschwitz.

The judges awarded me the prize. They did not publish the piece because it was fiction. It had broken the rules. But are not rules made to be broken? How many rules did Teta break to save the lives of eight people?

Then, one fine day, many years later, I read Eva Gossman's story. It is one of my tasks, perhaps a duty, possibly a *mitzva*, to read the stories of Holocaust survivors. I have read scores, probably over a hundred. They come in all sorts and styles. Few, if any, are written as well as Eva's. Eva's account is beautifully written. It has life and soul in it: Eva's life and soul.

Even if it were poorly written, we would have to have it, need to read it: for Teta's sake.

Imagine me turning the pages that fine day. Here was Presov. Here was a righteous Gentile. Here at the cash desk of the *mikva* in Presov was a Gentile as righteous as any. She did not have to be invented. Her sturdy independence of mind and spirit did not have to be imagined. Fact is superior to fiction.

I was elated. Came close to levitating. Instead, I wrote to Eva enclosing the story of Janko M. Who prefigured whom? Mária K. had a daughter, Vlasta. If she had had a son, would he not have been Janko? Or was Janko Mária's elder brother?

Eva was pleased to find her Slovak town on my map, her Teta in my Janko: if that is not too presumptuous a transmutation. What would Teta have made of Janko? Eva will one day tell me. Meanwhile she has allowed me to write this Foreword. It is not a duty, not a *mitzva*, simply (and absolutely) a privilege.

So Presov does exist. In Prague recently I bought a new guide to Slovakia (getting a sharp look from the Czech shop assistant). In it Presov has ten pages. There is no mention of Jews in the brief history of the town. No mention of Mária Krescanková, righteous Slovak, either. The synagogue is shown on the town plan and receives a few lines in the gazetteer: the most beautiful synagogue in Slovakia still in use.

Yet, it is no use pretending. The life has gone out of east and central Europe. We all know it. The ghosts are more alive than the living. Every forest clearing has its unbearable memories. Every street has its washed-out bloodstains. Against every wall someone was stood to be shot.

They will tell you: there is nothing there. There always is. Half a tombstone, a broken bowl, bullet marks in the prayer house wall, a dip in the ground, a layer of ash, different flora and fauna.

Looking at the photographs of Roman Vishniac, reading Patrick Leigh Fermor or Gregor von Rezzori, thinking about the pluralistic world they convey so vividly, what are we to think? What are we to imagine?

Fortunately, we do not have to imagine Teta. She lived. She saved lives. Blessed be she. And it is a blessing too, if of a different sort, to have Eva Gossman's story. Books too will pass away. Do they survive longer than memory does?

Eva's account of Teta touches on eternity: eternal values, eternal truths. Her book brings Teta to life; it makes Mária K. live in our minds. I hope that means forever.

Colin Richmond
London 2002

1 To Write or Not to Write?

I was eight years old when the war started in the fall of 1939 and 14 when it ended for us in April 1945. I have spent most of my life in ordinary pursuits – going to school, choosing a profession, getting married, raising a child, forming friendships and, to the best of my ability, contributing modestly to the welfare of the communities in which I have lived. Over the years, memories of the past have become progressively dimmer. I believed that the person I had become owed much more to the reality of the present, and the promise of the future, than to a distant, half forgotten past.

Yet even when I was totally absorbed in meeting new challenges and seeking new opportunities, when I was happy and fulfilled, when I rushed toward a future which at times seemed limitless, part of me continued to look backwards. What I wanted to preserve was not the horror of the war, the enormity of our individual and collective losses, or the pain of survival. Rather, I struggled to save from oblivion the deeds of a handful of people without whose help neither my family nor I would have survived. Buried under the distractions of a busy life was the knowledge that, some day, I would write an account of the actions of a few individuals whose efforts and interventions saved us from the fate of the more than 90,000 Jews who had lived in Slovakia at the beginning of the war. Almost all were deported to concentration camps, and more than 80 per cent perished. In my imagination, the book was to be not a personal memoir, but a humble tribute to those who gave me a second chance at life.

And yet, now that I have the leisure to act on my resolve, I have great ambivalence about fulfilling the promise I made to myself. Trying to understand this ambivalence may well be part of the story I tell.

There are powerful reasons for *not* writing this book. Some are general, others more personal. None of them occurred to me

1

before I was ready to start writing. Perhaps over the years I derived comfort from the prospect of writing the book, and I was not prepared to entertain challenges. Conversely, I might have feared that thinking about the difficulties would provide an excuse for not writing. But now, just as I am about to embark on this journey of discovery and rediscovery, I must listen to the voices that caution against undertaking it.

Given the proliferation of books about the Holocaust, one has to ask whether it is sensible – or perhaps even seemly – to write one more account of that period. Even if its purpose is not to recount the horrors of those years or the sufferings of individuals, but to pay tribute to a few extraordinary men and women, the story has to be set in its broader historical and familial context. It thus, inevitably, becomes part of 'Holocaust literature' , or more specifically, 'Holocaust memoir literature'. On one level, the question is about the utility of the endeavour: can a personal narrative add something that might enlarge our understanding or shed new light on the events? Will it help future historians to understand how the events they write about were 'lived' by individuals, in the ways that slave narratives give us a deeper and richer understanding of slavery in the United States? Will my account become part of a mosaic that gives texture to the broad strokes of social and political history, or will it just repeat a tale that has been told repeatedly?

Beyond the question of utility lurks a deeper concern. By writing one more account of a historical period that has received so much attention, and one more account of the heroism of a few, might one not, however unwittingly, contribute to the trivialization of both good and evil? Is there something new and important that has been left unsaid? Or does the repetition of the story dull both our interest and our sensibilities? Have we heard it too many times and are we becoming tired and bored listening to it?

Given the enormity of the subject one must also ask whether, by writing one more book on the Holocaust experience, one is complicit in creating the impression that what happened can be 'tamed', comprehended and transformed into a story. Will it contribute to an understanding of the Holocaust, with its villains, its spectators and its very few heroes, or will it blur the distinctions among them? Will it help, in its own small way, to

2

present the Holocaust as just another slice of historical reality, as seen from multiple perspectives? Would I contribute to efforts to reduce what may have been a unique moment of evil, when the powers of advanced industrialization were harnessed by a zealous and efficient bureaucracy for purposes of mass extermination, to a comprehensible period of human history? And even if this will inevitably happen at some future time (and perhaps it should happen), should I play any part in this transformation of events which I experienced as great catastrophes and thus contribute, however modestly, to the domestication of evil?

The second concern deals with the reliability of memory more than 50 years after the events, as well as with the hazards of selective memory. Forgetting is an adaptive feature of memory – we inevitably select what we remember from the past in order to have the courage to face the future. The more difficult the memories, the greater the impetus to bury them. When we embark on what resembles an archaeological excavation of a buried private realm, we may construct as much as we reconstruct; we may repair as much as we portray. Do we compose the narratives of memories from fragmented remains of our past, or do we have privileged, even if only limited, access to events that affected us deeply long ago? Do we create order and coherence, or do we find it? How significantly is our autobiographical memory affected by our life experiences and by our need to elaborate and make sense out of the broken chips that remain of events and experiences? How much poetic license are we allowed to fill in the empty spaces, to make our story more engaging, or more credible? How do we calibrate the permissible distance from both history and fiction?

And the questions continue on a more personal level. Will the focus on those who saved us blur the pain and suffering that was the harsh reality of our daily lives? And if writing about selected and in some ways disconnected events of our lives does not improve our comprehension of the historical past, will it at least lead to better self-understanding? Perhaps, but then one has to ask, 'What is the price of self-understanding?' What are the hazards of stepping out of a life of 'laughter and forgetting' into a life filled with grief and loss? It is impossible to remember the good without the evil, and it is impossible to accurately render the depth of the evil when it is illuminated by the good. Will

3

the recollection of evil bring darkness and pain? These are questions that give me pause. Yet they cannot be answered in advance, before the task is accomplished, and by then it may be too late. Having seen the light of day, the genie will refuse to go back into the bottle.

Finally, I question my ability to write the kind of book I have always intended to write. I know that I do not want to write a book about myself, but about the people who helped us. Will I succeed in telling their story without placing my family or myself in the limelight? I have read many moving accounts written by survivors who were children during the Second World War. Some of them captured with great eloquence and clarity the perspective of a child caught in circumstances that defy even adult understanding. These narratives direct our attention not so much to the events that are happening on the outside, but to the complexity of the children's interpretations of what is happening to them, to their resilience in coping with traumatic events and to their adaptability to new, strange and often very harsh circumstances. Then there are books that talk about the scars left by these traumatic childhood experiences and about their re-emergence, at unexpected times and in unlikely places, in the lives of the adults. All of these are important books, but they are not models for what I want to do. The story I want to tell is not about a child, or even a family, that survived the war, but about the people without whose help and intervention all of us would have perished. It is their lives and actions I want to record and celebrate. But it is hard to do them justice and to assign them the place of honour they deserve. In real life we owe our survival to them; yet in the story I tell, their actions can be understood only in the context of our family history. In my heart, they are the heroes who occupy centre stage; in my story, they are actors in a drama that encompasses not only our family, but also the Jewish community of Prešov. The clarity of their moral actions may at times be blurred in the midst of the narrative of our everyday lives and struggles before, during and after the war.

There are also good reasons for writing the book. I find three of them most compelling.

The first general reason is reflected in the title of the book – *Good Beyond Evil*. According to Jewish legend, every generation

4

is saved by the presence of 36 righteous people who go unrecognized and uncelebrated as they live their unremarkable and often modest, private lives. While the story of the Holocaust (despite the work of a few contemporary revisionist historians who question its veracity) has a secure place in history and will continue to be told, in many voices and from many perspectives, the story of those exceptional individuals who maintained the light of humanity when the rest of the world was plunged into darkness may easily be forgotten. They live primarily in the memory of those whom they saved and in the stories they tell. Their presence is fragile and fleeting. The major theme of the period has to be the evil master plan executed on an unprecedented scale with fanatical zeal, bureaucratic efficiency and industrial might; the minor theme has to include the presence of those who defied evil and who, through their acts, affirmed not only the humanity of those they saved, but the humanity of all of us. These extraordinary individuals, who chose to be neither perpetrators nor bystanders, and who risked everything to save a few, should not remain anonymous or be relegated to footnotes in the larger historical narrative. The standard they set for what is possible should inform our assessment of the past and our expectations of the future. It must enter our historical, political and moral vocabulary.

II   The second reason for writing this book is to reaffirm one of my deepest convictions: that we bear personal responsibility for our acts, regardless of whether they are good, bad or morally neutral. While our choices may be severely circumscribed by our historical, social, political and economic circumstances, by our educational backgrounds as well as by our genetic markers, we are not deprived of our ability to make choices. Our claim to being human is based on our willingness to take responsibility for our acts – even as we recognize that our lives have boundaries and that our freedom has limits. To say that we cannot choose the circumstances under which we are compelled to act does not mean that we have no choice about how we act in the circumstances in which we find ourselves. It is true that modern totalitarian regimes try to enforce their absolute dominion over all aspects of their citizens' lives through the use of extensive neighbourhood spying systems as a strategy for obliterating any demarcations between public and private spheres.

While tyrants and dictators mete out harsh, swift and public punishment to those who protest or transgress even the most insignificant edict (on the premise that absolute power must never be challenged), they also ensure compliance through the use of seductive rhetoric, sanctioned violence, endless incantations and ceremonial magic. Yet the claim that one is a helpless prisoner of the 'system' and its institutions is belied both by our ordinary moral vocabulary and by the acts of those few who, at the risk of their lives, throw off their chains. Corrupt institutions and corrupt bureaucracies may put severe constraints on our lives, but they do not deprive us of our ability to make choices.

Our choices have consequences – good or bad, intended or unintended, foreseen or unforeseen. They may be easy or they may be difficult; they may bring condemnation or approbation; they may involve glory or defeat; they may be based on a great deal of reflection or spurred by an immediate impulse. Whatever they are, and however we make them, our choices do not only define the quality of our individual lives; they also have an effect, minuscule as it may be, on the course of history. However much we might believe that vast impersonal forces determine historical events, it is impossible to make sense out of the past without giving weight to the intervention of individual actors – some performing on the world stage, most toiling in their private and communal worlds.

The more specific reason for writing the book has to do with the individuals about whom I want to write. I cannot repay the debt I owe them, but I can acknowledge it publicly. They never thought of themselves as heroes, and they certainly were not heroes in their own communities. During the war, they were enemies of the 'law' and of the 'state,' subject to harassment by neighbours, betrayal by informers and death at the hands of the Nazi collaborators and the local police. At best they were unpatriotic, at worst they were traitors. After the war, they were commonly viewed with suspicion, either because they were thought to have obtained material rewards from those they saved (greed being more comprehensible than altruism) or, even more perniciously, because they robbed the Final Solution of its ultimate success. As the years went by, they largely resumed their ordinary lives, becoming indistinguishable from the rest of their community. Those whom they saved often emigrated to

6

new places to forget the past and to start new lives. *Remembering* [handwritten note: *Remembering*]
Remembering the past was too dangerous for the rescuers and
too painful for the rescued. In another few years, neither the
one, nor the other, will be alive, and memories of the events that [handwritten note: *future*]
bound them together will die with them. Histories will continue
to be written, but will stories continue to be told? Even if they
are, they will be crafted by writers, poets and musicians whose
own lives are distant from the events they describe, for audi-
ences who themselves are living in a different historical reality.

There were five people – four adults and one child – who
saved my life and the lives of my parents, my brother and sister
and a cousin: a young woman we called '*Teta*' (aunt in Slovak)
and her 11-year-old daughter; a grocer and his wife who were
our next door neighbours while we were in hiding in a provincial town in the south-western part of Slovakia; and a chambermaid in a local hotel. They are the heroes of our story. Then
there are five other people whom I want to acknowledge: two
members of the Russian Army – one a Jewish officer, the other a
military doctor; an adventurer of uncertain nationality; a crazed
survivor of a concentration camp; and a Carmelite nun. They
entered our lives suddenly, unexpectedly, and for only brief
moments. They were not directly involved in our rescue and we
would have survived without their interventions. Nevertheless,
their actions brought light and kindness into our otherwise
bleak existence. Measured by ordinary standards, what they did
may appear quite unremarkable – but the intensity and vividness with which I remember them today, 56 years after the
events, attest to their significance in the life of a hunted and persecuted child. They, too, affirmed good beyond evil.

2 End of Childhood

Our relatively peaceful middle class existence in Prešov, a medium sized industrial town in the eastern part of Slovakia, ended in the spring of 1939, when Slovakia became an independent state, headed by a Catholic priest, Monsignor Jozef Tiso.

Before the partition of Czechoslovakia, about 135,000 Jews, roughly 4.5 per cent of the population, lived in Slovak territories. Close to one third of them had their homes in hamlets, villages and provincial towns in the easternmost corner of Slovakia, in the Ruthenian and Subcarpathian regions, which were ceded to Hungary in 1939. Eager to reduce the Jewish population after Slovakia became an independent state, Tiso and his government ordered the forceful removal of most of the Jews who lived in the territories adjoining the readjusted borders with Hungary, along with those who claimed Hungarian citizenship, into the no man's land separating the two countries. The expulsion, carried out under inhuman conditions, left a large number of people stranded without adequate food or shelter. Some were sent off to labour camps, others were eventually absorbed in Hungary and Romania; most of them ultimately perished in concentration camps. About 90,000 Jews remained in Slovakia – roughly 3 per cent of the Slovak population. But even after the ruthless 'cleansing' of the border territories which, in ways we did not understand then, foreshadowed the brutality of the newly established regime, no one could have imagined, at the start of World War II, that fewer than 20 per cent of the remaining Jews would survive the war.

The Prešov of my childhood was a pleasant and prosperous city of 60,000 inhabitants. A lively commercial centre with broad avenues, countless city squares, handsome architecture and an active cultural life, its 6,000 Jews participated in the life of the city as well as in their own communal and religious affairs. Only with hindsight can one describe the geographical location of the

HISTORICAL
BCK GROUND

city in a far more sinister way – as a place within driving distance of six death camps: Auschwitz, Belzec, Chelmo, Majdanek, Sobibor and Treblinka.

It is relatively easy to sketch the political events that dominated our existence during the six years of Slovak independence. With the final break up of Czechoslovakia on 14 March 1939, and the election of Father Jozef Tiso as head of state, Slovakia became an ally of Nazi Germany, while the Czech lands and Moravia became a German 'protectorate'. One of the first acts of the Slovak state (23 March 1939) was to sign a 'Treaty of Protection' (*Schutzvertrag*) with the German foreign minister, Joachim von Ribbentrop, which allowed the German Reich to determine the foreign policy of Slovakia and to interfere with domestic issues, of which the most prominent was 'the Jewish question'.

3/14/39

2/23

The dismemberment of the Czechoslovak Republic had, in fact, started six months earlier, on 29 September 1938, when, by the terms of the Munich Agreement, the northern part of Bohemia, known as Sudetenland, was ceded to Germany as ransom for 'peace in our time'. A few weeks later, Slovakia became an autonomous state within Czecho-Slovakia. Born with a great deal of promise and hope at the end of the First World War, Czechoslovakia died before the first shots of the Second World War were fired.

Much more difficult to recapture, almost 60 years after the events, are the alternating moods of dread and hope that permeated our everyday lives; or the strategies of accommodation and resistance we developed and perfected over time; or even the losses and the sorrows that dominated all aspects of our existence. The destruction of the Jewish community of Prešov took five years (1939–1944) and the full legal basis for the persecutions was codified only in September 1941, three months after Slovakia officially entered the war on 21 June 1941. The 'Jewish Codex' explicitly defined Jews as a racial group, physiologically and psychologically different from the rest of the population. However, persecutions and harassment started almost immediately after the declaration of Slovak independence. Decrees excluding Jews from business, the professions and government service came in rapid succession. We felt besieged; outcasts in our own country and among our own people. Each day we read

5 yr 5

Jewish Codex

Common elements in 'theocratic" let-the newspapers, listened to the radio and scanned the anti-Jewish announcements posted on street kiosks, hoping against hope for a reprieve. We knew about *Kristallnacht* in Germany (9–10 November 1938) and had some inkling about what was happening in Nazi-occupied Poland, but, at least in the beginning, we put on blinders, perhaps to give ourselves the courage and the resourcefulness to go on. Clarity of vision might have resulted in a paralyzing despair, or it might have spurred us to action, even if it involved uprooting ourselves and fleeing to any country that would have us.

In hindsight, it may be difficult to understand why the Jews, in Germany and in the collaborating or occupied countries, did not read the handwriting on the wall much earlier and leave while they could still get out, with or without their possessions, however circumscribed their options might have been. At least in the beginning, there were compelling reasons for staying and 'waiting things out', and we were persuaded by them. The history of Jews is filled with periods of harsh measures and expulsions, followed by more benign treatment over relatively long stretches of time. Would the Angel of Death pass by and leave us bruised, but alive? There was a certain randomness about the laws targeting the Jews which provided sufficient breathing spells to make the situation appear, even once the deportations started, less than hopeless. Unfortunately, there was no full dress rehearsal before the Final Solution. And there was no script that could warn us of the difference between persecutions on a local scale, or even the larger, organized pogroms of the past, and the well laid government plans, developed and refined over close to a decade, which aimed at the total annihilation of all the Jews who lived in any corner of the Third Reich or its satellites. Finally, as the intensity of the persecutions increased, the opportunities for leaving no longer existed. Even if we could still get out, there was no place that would let us in. By the terms of the Evian Conference convened by Roosevelt in July 1938 (four months before *Kristallnacht*), no Western country would be expected to adjust its immigration laws to allow for the influx of Jewish refugees from all parts of Europe. Between 1933 and 1938, close to 320,000 Jews left Germany. Roughly half of them went to the United States (102,000) and Great Britain (52,000). Other favoured destinations were Argentina (63,000),

South Africa (36,000), Palestine (33,000), Australia (8,600) and Canada (6,000). Only about 7,000 made it next door to Switzerland (source: Sir Martin Gilbert, *Atlas of the Holocaust*). These figures do not include the roughly 10,000 children from Germany, Austria and Czechoslovakia who left on the *Kindertransport* for England between 1938 and 1939. In light of later developments that made Japan and Germany war time allies, it is ironic that the Japanese Government allowed somewhere between 17,000 and 18,000 Jewish refugees to settle in the occupied city of Shanghai in 1938. For the Jews of Prešov, Shanghai was on the other side of the moon.

However bad the situation was in 1939 and 1940, much worse was to come. And most of us were not prepared. Even if we did not despair in the early days, it is puzzling that we continued to hope. Did we believe that even if things did not improve, they would at least not get worse? Did we expect that there would be some sort of magical line at which the persecutions would halt? Or did we expect a swift defeat of Germany or the intervention of the rest of the world on our behalf? Assessing the gradual unfolding of events from the secure position of the present, we may have to accept the fact that we suffered from a lack of imagination about the depth of depravity and inhumanity with which a legitimately constituted government could act against its own citizens. The Jews of Slovakia, and those in most other countries occupied or allied with the Reich, paid a high price for living with hope. But the perfect vision we may acquire in examining the past does not extend into seeing the future.

Tiso's chief qualification for the presidency came from his position as head of the Hlinka Slovak Peoples' Party, a strongly nationalistic and rabidly anti-Semitic political party established by the Catholic priest, Andrej Hlinka, in 1918 to oppose the newly created Czechoslovak Republic. Tiso's political platform incorporated the ideals of the Hlinka party and had two major planks: political independence from the Czech Republic and the elimination of Jews from all aspects of Slovak life. Anti-Semitism and nationalism were deeply intertwined, both in the minds of the majority of the population and in the new laws of the land. Jews, dangerous and implacable enemies of the newly created Slovak state, had to be dealt with harshly and decisively. The accusations levelled against the Jews were much the same as

11

those propagated by the Nazi government in Germany. They were internationalists, capitalists, communists, cosmopolitans and world conspirators. They were vultures and parasites who fed on the innocent. Their uncompromising goal was world domination. Because of the deep religious roots of the Hlinka party (about 70 per cent of the population of Slovakia was Roman Catholic), the Jews were also portrayed as the killers of Christ, with frequent references to the ritual killings perpetrated by them on young Christian boys and girls. The myth of ritual murder was deeply embedded in the minds of the citizens of Czechoslovakia, often supported by the teachings of the Church. The Jews, as the tale was told over and over again, used the blood of young Christians in the preparation of their Passover *matzoh*. The Tiso government did not have to invent the charge – only to resurrect it. Doctrinal anti-Semitism nourished the secular anti-Semitism of the state.

One of the staunchest defenders of Jews against the ritual murder accusations was the first President of Czechoslovakia, Thomáš Garrigue Masaryk. As a young professor of philosophy at the Czech University of Prague, he came publicly to the defence of an itinerant cobbler and peddler, Leopold Hilsner, who in 1898 was accused of the ritual murder of a young woman, Anežka Hrúžová. When the verdict, sentencing Hilsner to death, was annulled, the prosecutor demanded another trial which included charges of ritual murder in the death of yet another young woman, Maria Klimová. Masaryk again spoke out, in lectures and in the press, not only against the specific charges levelled against Hilsner, but more broadly against the myth of ritual murder and the anti-Semitism that fuelled the charges and enjoyed the support of many Czech intellectuals, as well as of the Church. He paid dearly for his position, including a boycott of his university lectures orchestrated by some of his students. But his voice was not lost in the wilderness. With moral indignation, strengthened by medical and forensic research, Masaryk exposed the trumped up nature of the charges. His efforts were not immediately successful and the verdict at the end of the second trial condemned Hilsner to life imprisonment. Yet, like Zola's defence of Captain Dreyfus around the same time, his fight against anti-Semitism in general, and the charge of ritual murder in particular, was not in vain.

Almost two decades after the Hilsner conviction, another Jew, Mendel Bejlis, was brought to trial in Kiev on charges of having perpetrated the ritual murder of a young Russian boy. This time the trial produced an outcry in Vienna and Prague, and many Czechs signed a resolution, promoted by Masaryk, condemning the lack of judicial process. The document became the platform for a broader attack on the myth of ritual murder.

As a university professor and philosopher, Masaryk fought anti-Semitism in its many guises. When he became President of Czechoslovakia, he continued to use his voice and his pen in the cause he had first embraced 20 years earlier. He now had the moral authority, the power and the platform to work for the establishment of institutional and legal safeguards against persecution and discrimination, which became the cornerstone of the fledgling republic. Masaryk died in 1937, and was spared the spectacle of official and ruthless anti-Semitism in his own country. With the collapse of Czechoslovakia, anti-Semitism surfaced again, nourished by the teachings of the Church and the prejudices and xenophobia of the inhabitants of the Czech and Slovak lands.

Despite the deep roots of anti-Semitism in the region, it is important to reflect on the relationship between the historical and clerical anti-Semitism endemic in Slovak society, and the promulgation of a policy of total annihilation. The basis of doctrinal anti-Judaism was the refusal of Jews to accept the divinity of Christ. Those who converted were welcomed by the Church and accepted into the community of believers (at least after one generation of being good Christians). The historical basis of anti-Semitism was a blend of theological hatreds and secular grievances. While most Slovaks applauded the efforts to isolate Jews from civic society and were eager to profit from their persecutions, it is not clear how many of them wished for, or participated actively in, the extermination of the Jews. If they wanted them out of their towns and villages and were eager to deprive them of their possessions, they did not necessarily want them dead. The leaders of Slovakia, with the help of their German advisers, exploited the theological and historical anti-Semitism when they adopted the Nazi plan of the Final Solution. The Jews were demonized and degraded, depicted as racially and morally inferior; a cancer on the body politic. The health and even survival of the nation demanded that they be exterminated.

13

medical terminology
+ antisemetic propaganda

The use of medical terminology for political purposes proved to be brilliant and persuasive. In the Nazi repertoire, health was defined as absence of illness and could only be achieved by the surgical excision of Jews and other undesirables from society. It is instructive to note that the medical profession was deeply involved in executing, if not drafting, Nazi policies right from the beginning. Without the co-operation of many physicians, it would have been impossible to implement the eugenics programme of 'racial purification' initiated by the Nazi government against its own population well before the articulation of the Final Solution. Hundreds of thousands of individuals who suffered from hereditary disease or mental illness were killed or forcibly sterilized (Christopher Browning gives the figures of 400,000 sterilized and 100,000 subjected to euthanasia by gas or lethal injection) and many families, regardless of race or religion, received deceptive death certificates for their institutionalized relatives. A few years later, doctors participated actively in the 'selection process', which condemned the very young, the sick and the weak to extermination as soon as they passed the gates of the concentration camps; and they designed and conducted unspeakably cruel medical experiments on captive populations. The German doctors had a great deal to answer for at the end of the war. (My subsequent professional interest in medical ethics came from reading the transcripts of the 1946–49 Nuremberg trials of the 23 German doctors who stood accused of 'crimes against humanity', in addition to the specific charges read against each one.) The experiments they conducted were inhumane in their design and apparently useless either in advancing medical research, or in helping the war effort. Two of the most telling defence strategies were to point out that the findings based on these experiments had been published in respected and widely distributed academic journals and that no objections had been raised against them; and, further, that medical experiments had been routinely conducted on native populations by colonial powers or by sovereign states on their own incarcerated populations.

When Tiso came to power, the Jews were immediately targeted as a political, economic, physical and spiritual threat to the newly established republic – with the spectre of ritual murder as the bloodiest, and most inflammatory charge. In retrospect, his intentions should have been clear when one of the first acts of his government, in the spring of 1939, was to establish a Department of Jewish Affairs; a code name for an institutional entity charged with the responsibility of overseeing the elimination of Jews from Slovak national life. A year later, in August of 1940, Dieter Wisličeny, Eichmann's deputy, arrived in Bratislava to advise the Department of Jewish Affairs.

With Tiso at the helm, and a cabinet that included the pro-Nazi, Vojtek Tuka, as Prime Minister and Šaňo Mach, the head of the Hlinka Guard, it should not have come as a surprise that Slovak independence was, from its very beginnings, celebrated with a series of specific and harsh measures against the Jews. Jews' monthly incomes were limited to a set amount; ownership of Jewish businesses had to be passed to 'Aryans'; Jewish children could not attend public schools; Jews were forbidden to participate in any civic activities or to attend public functions. Law did not guarantee their physical safety and their property could be expropriated on the flimsiest excuse. The confiscated property was often distributed to the citizens as a gesture of 'good will'. The prohibitions and exclusions were designed to isolate Jews as much as possible from the life of the community, to disrupt their daily lives, to deprive them of their livelihood, to constrain their movements and to offer them as scapegoats for whatever social and economic problems the newly created republic might experience. Jews were frequently the victims of random violence and their homes could be looted with impunity.

To strengthen his popular base, Tiso gave official status to a paramilitary group created after the First World War to serve the goals of the Christian Slovak Peoples' Party, and called it, appropriately, the Hlinka Guard. Not only did they enforce the official edicts against the Jews with unspeakable cruelty and zeal, they frequently took the law into their own hands, especially during the brief moments of respite from German initiated or government sponsored persecutions. We feared them more than the dreaded SS. They were omnipresent, violent, lawless and arbitrary. They travelled in groups and hunted without mercy. Their songs, their parades, their speeches and their posturing gave them the courage to kill and conferred on their acts of torture a ceremonial and festive air. Thus, two years after it came into existence, the Slovak state was fully equipped for the persecution of the Jews. It had an ideology that demanded it, a government agency that oversaw it, a legal framework that justified it and an internal military force that, with the blessing of the German Government, would enforce it.

The provisions of the Jewish Codex, issued by the Slovak cabinet four months before the Wannsee Conference, which took place on 20 January 1942, may have exceeded in their harshness the Nuremberg laws (1933/1935.) The Codex was written in the shadow of the Final Solution, at a time when the German Government was moving from a policy of forced emigration, expulsion, labour camps, and resettlement of Jews, to one that aimed at their total annihilation in all parts of the Third Reich and its satellite states. Although the planning for the Holocaust started in the late summer and early fall of 1941, the explicit programme for the extermination of all Jews under German domination (except for the '*Mischlinge*', who were to be sterilized) was fully articulated in the Wannsee Protocols. Under the terms of the Protocols, Jews were to be subjected to harsh labour that only few could survive. Those who did not succumb to 'natural causes' would have to be killed, since otherwise the 'survival of the fittest' would leave a nucleus for the regeneration of the race. The goal was to leave the expanded German Reich *Judenfrei*.

By classifying Jews as a racially inferior and undesirable minority, the Codex legitimized their forcible separation from the rest of the Slovak population. With a stroke of the pen, Jews were excluded from all participation in the economic and cultural life of the country. Even more important, they were deprived of any legal recourse against arbitrary acts of violence and humiliation perpetrated with government sanction, or at least without government interference, upon individuals or communities. The separate legislative edicts, promulgated over the previous two and a half years and enforced somewhat haphazardly, were now codified and made into the law of the land. Jews could not practice their profession; they were confined to their homes from seven in the evening until seven in the morning; they were moved from their apartments if they fronted any main thoroughfare; and they had to wear a yellow armband, exactly 3.9 inches in diameter with a one inch Star of David in the centre. Neither the very old, nor the very young, were exempt. To go out without the armband was to risk bodily harm, arrest and even deportation. Jews were an impure and parasitic race. With a perverse logic befitting a totalitarian government, Jews were declared liable for forced labour to help their country. Although they could not be trusted to serve in the armed forces, they were drafted into auxiliary labour units of the Slovak armed forces and obliged to make a contribution to the national effort to support the Axis.

While the Slovak Government enacted its own anti-Jewish legislation, the Jews of the Czech protectorate fell under the jurisdiction of the Reich and hence were subject to the Nuremberg laws. Substantively, there may not have been much difference between the laws of the Reich as they had evolved by 1941 and those of the Codex, and the daily lives of the Jews in the protectorate were not significantly better than those of the Jews of Slovakia. What may have been different was the ferocity with which the laws were executed by the local agencies and the degree to which they enlisted the co-operation of the general population. But in the end, both communities were decimated, with a somewhat smaller percentage of survivors in the protectorate.

By the fall of 1941 the political, economic, social and legal isolation of the Jews in Slovakia was complete. We lived in fear of the present and dread of the future. And yet there was an enormous struggle to keep some semblance of ordinary life. 'This is as bad as it can possibly get' were words frequently offered as consolation and reassurance. I remember hushed conversations in our living room; visits from friends; card games played after the curfew hours, with guests occasionally staying overnight to avoid being caught on the streets; and muffled laughter that followed the telling of a joke, even if it was gallows humour. A book of Jewish jokes, '*Frisch, Gesund and Meshuge*' (roughly: Perky, Healthy and Crazy), was our prized possession. It survived the war with us.

Much has been written about the role and limits of humour as a means of understanding, or even responding to, the events of the Holocaust. In dealing with large-scale catastrophes, is humour ever appropriate, or is it always in bad taste? Does humour diminish the victim, the perpetrator, and above all, the seriousness of the crimes? Can laughter ever be a suitable response to evil? And who is entitled to use humour? Is it per-

17

missible in some situations, and not in others, by some people
and not by others? Whatever position one may take on this issue
and however nuanced an answer one may offer, I know that our
little Jewish joke book relieved tension and provided solace. We
certainly did not take our situation lightly; we did not laugh at
ourselves or at our enemies. We laughed because, through
laughter, we affirmed our human capacity to look at life in ways
that eluded the power of our oppressors.

Massive deportations of the Jews of Slovakia occurred in
three waves. Between March and October 1942, nearly 75 per
cent of the Jews living in Slovakia were deported, some to labour
camps, most to the Auschwitz concentration camp. By the winter of 1942, fewer than 1,000 Jews were left in Prešov. The second
wave occurred in the summer of 1943, when every few weeks
Jews were rounded up randomly and transported to concentration camps. The final roundup of Slovak Jews (when none were
left in Prešov) occurred in the late fall of 1944, after the failure of
the Slovak partisan uprising in Banská Bystrica. By then, the
Germans and their allies knew that they had lost the war on the
battlefields, but they were relentless in their determination to
win the war against the Jews. It is hard to know whether they
were driven by a lust for vengeance on their victims, by a determination to complete the Final Solution and leave the territories
that once belonged to them *Judenfrei*, or by a desire to eliminate
every last witness to their atrocities; to rob them not only of their
lives, but also of their history. Whatever their aims, even during
the final months of the war, there was no letup in the ferocity of
the persecutions. Thousands died during the 'death marches' in
the spring of 1945, as they were forced to evacuate a soon to be
liberated concentration camp and move to one at some distance
from the advancing armies.

****

Our family life was closely intertwined with the life of the
Orthodox Jewish community of Prešov. My father, after working
briefly in his family's lumber business, was appointed, at the age
of thirty-one, *Notár* of the *Kehilla*: the legally incorporated Jewish
community in Prešov. The position, roughly equivalent to

'Executive Director', had evolved over time from a largely book-keeping and record gathering post to one that served increasingly as the focus for the interactions of the various institutions under the Jewish community umbrella – the synagogues, schools, ritual bath, burial society, etc. The *Notár* also represented the Jewish community in its interactions with state and local officials. My father was the last *Notár* of the Jewish community of Prešov.

Since the founding of Czechoslovakia, the Jews were recognized either as a nationality, or as a religious minority, both with full rights and privileges of citizenship. (In the 1930 census, about 63 per cent claimed Jewish nationality and about 37 per cent claimed Slovak nationality.) The majority of Jews were members of the orthodox Jewish community.

Our childhood was spent in the courtyard of the Jewish community complex (which included a synagogue, a school, offices and living quarters for some employees), where we played with the children of other employees and members. It was not a ghetto, but the centre of our social life. Our home was bilingual – occasionally trilingual. Our parents spoke German with each other, with most of their friends and with their children. We spoke German with our parents and grandparents, and Slovak with each other, in school and with our friends. Some of our relatives spoke Hungarian. None of us knew Yiddish, although we could more or less understand it as a variation of German. We were not an assimilated family, and our lives were governed by religious traditions, rituals and learning. We had our share of rabbis, but also of doctors and lawyers. My mother's father, although an orthodox rabbi in Hamburg, Germany, had earned a doctorate in philosophy under the tutelage of Wilhelm Wundt (1832–1920). His doctoral thesis was an analysis and critique of Wundt's ethics (somewhat to the discomfort of his teacher, who is said to have remarked that he expected something better from his prize student). My father attended business school in Berlin and many of my uncles entered the professions. We lived our lives both as Jews and as citizens of Czechoslovakia.

In a brief introduction to a pamphlet my father wrote in 1940, in which he recounted the 70-year history of the orthodox Jewish community in Prešov (1871–1941; I am not sure how the date of publication can be prior to the last year covered in the narrative, unless it is not a full calendar year, but a fiscal year that started in 1940), he noted, with extreme circumspection, that due to the sad circumstances of the Jewish population in the last few years, the *Kehilla*, which heretofore was occupied almost exclusively with religious and cultural matters, now also had to assume responsibility for the social, economic and physical survival of the Jewish community. It had to attend to the needs of all Jews, regardless of their official membership status. Affiliation with the Jewish community was no longer either voluntary or religious in nature. It was decreed by the government and forced on all those who were classified as Jews under the Codex. As a 'race' (i.e. a group that shared physical and mental traits transmitted genetically or through tradition), and an undesirable one at that, individual Jews no longer had the freedom to determine who they were, what they believed and to what associations they wanted to belong. While his language was guarded, my father's message was clear. To be a Jew has ceased to be a matter of self-identification and has become a government designation. Whatever self-imposed lines of demarcation may have existed between Orthodox, Reform, totally assimilated and recently converted Jews (or even people with more than one Jewish grandparent), were erased by the stroke of a pen that defined all Jews as a separate racial group. The pamphlet is not only the record of the 70-year history of the Orthodox Jewish community of Prešov, but also its last chapter. A year later, the community ceased to exist. Ironically, more than 55 years after the war, in the fall of 1997, the meticulous restoration of the beautiful main synagogue of Prešov was celebrated with considerable fanfare and official participation. But the building is more a memory of the past than a promise for the future. The once thriving community of 6,000 now consists of about 60 elderly members whose families are scattered around the globe. It is hard to imagine that Prešov will ever again be a vital and energetic centre of Jewish communal life.

In September 1940, the year of the publication of the pamphlet, and a month after the arrival of Eichmann's deputy, Wisličeny, in Slovakia, the government established the *Ústredna Židov* (*ÚŽ*) in Bratislava, the capital of Slovakia. Superficially, the ÚŽ took over the functions of the *Kehilla*. More ominously, it became the only Jewish authority allowed to represent the Jews to the government, negotiate with the Department for Jewish Affairs, transmit government instructions to the Jews and ensure compliance with them. In February 1942, six months after the promulgation of the Codex and a month before the beginning of the first massive deportations of Jewish families, a branch of the ÚŽ office was opened in Prešov – here, too, superseding all other Jewish communal organizations. With the creation of the ÚŽ, Jewish communal life in Prešov was fundamentally transformed and its primary focus shifted from religious and spiritual concerns to concerns for the physical, economic, psychological and social survival of the community. The head of the ÚŽ no longer represented the interests and concerns of the *Kehilla*, made up of fully fledged citizens, to the government, but unhappily became the messenger, the negotiator, and at times even the enforcer, of government edicts.

Perhaps because he was the executive director of the Jewish community of Prešov, my father was asked to become the head of the newly created ÚŽ branch in Prešov. Deeply troubled by the prospect of a role he did not seek and one that inevitably involved serving as an intermediary between his community, the Slovak Government and the German 'advisors', he travelled to Bratislava to consult Rabbi Rafael Blum, his former teacher and mentor. He must have known how hard it would be to retain moral rectitude and a sense of justice in a position that was defined largely by those dedicated to the humiliation, harassment and impoverishment of his community. I do not think that at that point anyone really thought in terms of total annihilation. Despite his qualms and disquiet, he must also have known that by not accepting the position thrust upon him he would eliminate the possibility of helping, however marginally, the community he had served for many years. Whether he also thought that his position might shield his family to some degree I do not know. What I do know is that he could not save his mother or his siblings and their families from deportation; and that in the winter of 1942, after the first deportations from Slovakia, he had so little confidence in his ability to protect us that he sent my brother and me to Hungary to get us, at least temporarily, out of harm's way. I also know that his was a role he did not want. However morally troubling those years may have been for my father, both at the time and in retrospect, there is ample evidence that he had done the best he could under circumstances in which no human being should be tested. Shortly after the end of the war, he was elected to be the executive director of the Jewish community in Košice. A few years later, after he emigrated to Israel, he was elected to several successive terms as the mayor of Beer Yaacov, where he lived for close to 20 years, until his death in May 1970. Had his actions during the war been less then exemplary (no matter how difficult the decisions and how constrained the choices might have been), he would not have gained elective office first in post-war Czechoslovakia and then in Israel. Those who survived the war and returned to Slovakia, or emigrated to Israel, were not likely to have a forgiving or compassionate attitude toward officials who, for whatever reasons, were forced to have frequent interactions with the authorities in charge of persecutions and deportations. By electing my father to leadership positions, the survivors expressed their confidence that, after the horrors of the war, he could help them build, or rebuild, a community.

As head of the Prešov ÚŽ, my father's position may serve as a good example of what in political philosophy, is called the 'problem of dirty hands' – the pressure, under extreme conditions, to do bad things in order to accomplish a greater or more extensive good, or at least to ameliorate a worse outcome. A moral purist may reject a consequentialist calculus that accepts even a grave injustice for the sake of bringing about a more widely distributed benefit, but such judgements are bound to appear quite differently when all members of the community are threatened with annihilation and the immediate choice is between the very bad and the catastrophic. There is an extensive rabbinical literature dealing with the circumstances under which one is permitted, or even obliged, to meet the demands of a tyrant, a murderer or an enemy. This literature continued to provide moral guidance for the Jews, even in times of their most brutal oppression – in overcrowded ghettos, decimated communities and labour camps. It must have been under this rabbinic imprimatur that the so called 'Bratislava Working Group', headed by the Orthodox Rabbi, Chaim Weismandl, and his socialist Zionist cousin, Gisi Fleischmann, engaged in extensive bribery of local Nazi officials, as well as of the German representative to Slovakia, Dieter Wisličeny. Their efforts to protect the small remaining Jewish community of Slovakia from further deportations may have been partially successful. Deportations ceased between the summer of of 1942 and the spring of 1943. They started again in the summer of 1943, only to be suspended, without explanation, several weeks later. The same start and stop pattern was repeated in the spring of 1944. As late as the summer of 1944, the Bratislava Group attempted to extend its reach to Germany by offering Adolph Eichmann a 'trucks for Jews' deal in the hope of saving the Jews of Budapest. The morality of the rabbis required that no efforts be spared to save the lives of innocent men, women and children; the war aims of the Allies required that the enemy be deprived of even the most insignificant material benefits. The trucks were not delivered and the Jews of Budapest were not saved.

I wish my father and I had talked more about the war years – not only about events, but also about feelings, doubts, regrets, and lessons we might have learned. Although we visited each other regularly, the fact that I lived in America, and he in Israel, was at least a superficial impediment to spontaneous and intimate conversations. A deeper reason for avoiding discussions of the war years had to do with the reluctance experienced by many survivors to talk about the past. Those years were something we wanted to get away from, not resurrect. During the war we were reluctant to face the future; after the war, we avoided the past. We paid a price for these chronological interruptions – but they were the ransom we offered for our survival, first physically, by carrying out our daily tasks despite enormous pressures to give up, then psychologically, by creating a new life out of ashes.

Perhaps my life-long personal and professional interest in moral philosophy and applied ethics provides one strand of continuity between the events of my childhood and my adult life. During the war, good people were faced with bad choices and yet, all choices were not equally bad. Does a lesser evil become a good, even if only a conditional good? If so, is there an obligation to accept it and even work for it, or does one refuse, regardless of the consequences? Should moral categories retain their absolute character even in the face of their inevitable transgression under certain historical conditions, or should they allow for exceptions under extreme circumstances? And there

are many other, equally troubling questions of practical import.
Is one obliged to save a life even at the risk of losing one's own?
Can one continue to think in moral terms in an immoral world?
I believe one can. But the categories are less lucid and it would
be hard to claim that they are self-evident. Throughout the war,
we were faced with choices that might be hard to defend in a
safe and lawful world. Yet it would be wrong to conclude that
morality has no place under catastrophic conditions. On the
contrary, one has to continue to think in moral terms even if
one's acts are unavoidably tainted. I can only speculate whether
my father would have agreed with me, but I hope that he
would.

Obviously, Crossman is not telling something
about her father, or his position as leader
of UZ, which often had to be disseminator
of cruel edicts, & policies and even "Enforcers." ("messenger, negotiation,
even enforcer" p 21).

Crossman asks a series of difft
questions about the contradiction of
being a good person facing bad
choices & so forth.

How does this conflicting/Troubling
position apply to others of
the Jews who had compromise
thrust upon them? Say, the Catholic
regeme of Mrs. Tiso?

3 Family Fortunes: 1939–1945

The heroes of this book did not enter our lives until the late spring of 1944. Although I am eager to start their story, I believe it would be difficult to understand what they did, and how they did it, without some knowledge of our family circumstances between 1939 and 1944. The dire situation of the Jews in Slovakia, sketched in the previous chapter, provides the broader context for their deeds and attests to the exceptional character of their commitments. Yet the texture of their acts is intertwined with our lives in such intimate ways that it is impossible to understand them without the specificity of the situation in which we, and they, found ourselves.

My factual memories of the early years of the war are cloudy and fragmented, and I would be hard put to reconstruct our daily existence in a coherent narrative. What I have retained with far greater clarity are the emotions that dominated our existence – fear, anxiety, terror, sadness and disbelief. I can re-experience the feelings even as I no longer remember the events that occasioned them. And through these emotion-laden memories I can recall specific, unconnected events that do not add up to a complete story. Perhaps the most vivid, and most poignant among them, is of the time in the late spring of 1942, during the first wave of deportations of whole families from Prešov, when our very religious neighbour, Paiser Muller, came to say goodbye hours before he and his family had to report to the gathering grounds near the railroad which served as the staging area for the train rides to unknown destinations. He had many children, but the one I see most clearly was then about five years old, dressed in her best holiday outfit, dancing, prancing and singing in our living room. For her, wearing the blue velvet dress signified a happy, celebratory occasion. I do not know what explanation her parents gave her when, on an ordinary weekday, she was allowed to put on her Sabbath clothes. Did they believe, deeply and sincerely, that God would protect them from all harm, or did they do their utmost to shield their children from knowledge of a fate they themselves could only dimly comprehend? How long did her merriment last? How long before the little girl with almond eyes, curly hair and a smile on her face was separated from her parents and assigned to the hell reserved for small children?

I also remember the long evenings of curfews, when our parents and neighbours socialized and played cards to ward off boredom and to give a sense of normalcy to their abnormal situation. I remember the face of my father as he came home night after night with yet another bit of bad news. I can still hear the knock on our door and the shouting of orders on the day two SS men came to our apartment, at the time of the first deportations of unmarried young Jewish men and women in March 1942, looking for our Jewish maid, Fanny. She hid under the bed and, miraculously, was not caught. As in a Kafka tale, the great thoroughness with which the persecutors hunted their quarry turned out, at times, to be unaccountably sloppy, mocking their claim of absolute control over the destiny of each and every individual. But we knew that the search would be repeated on another day and that Fanny would not be lucky twice. That evening she left for a safer place. But safety in our circumstances was relative and temporary. We never saw her again, and I do not believe that she survived the war.

I can also hear the endless whispering of the adults in their frantic efforts to arrange phantom marriages (*Scheinehen*) between single young men and women to save them from becoming slave labourers in the work camps. To be sent to the camps was, for most people, tantamount to a death sentence. Letters written at great risk and smuggled out from time to time described the appalling conditions under which these labourers lived and the exceedingly high death rate among them. The stories told by the few who were lucky enough to escape from the camps confirmed and amplified the tales of horror. Their labour was cheap, their lives valueless. Only the hardiest had a chance to survive, and even then, not for long. Since the Slovak Government had exacted a promise from the Germans that the deported Jews would never return to Slovakia, the state could sell their properties for a fraction of their value to the local population. A secular version of indulgences!

Marriage, at least temporarily, exempted young people from the work camps. To my childish ears, these arranged marriages were quite romantic and I thought it was wonderful that adults encouraged young people to live together. I had neither the experience, nor the imagination, to understand the stresses and discomforts of these arrangements. I believe that only a few of these enforced marriages became permanent unions, even on the rare occasions when both partners survived the war.

Finally, I remember the accelerated activities in our household, combined with a great sense of hopelessness, when, in the late spring of 1942, the Germans and their Slovak allies started the deportations of all families who were not deemed economically essential to the state. Friends, relatives, neighbours and schoolmates disappeared from one day to the next, without warning and often without goodbyes. The transports were public, the grief private, the destination unknown.

In the winter of 1942, our situation was bleak and we could no longer pretend that perhaps the bad times would pass over, as they had done so often in the past. My father, reluctant to abandon the remnants of his community, nevertheless wanted to save his children. I am not sure how he arranged for our departure. I was told later that it was through a connection his younger sister, Ancsi, had with an official in the Hungarian police. I had just turned twelve and my brother was sixteen months older. We were joined by another Jewish youngster, whose name I do not remember. The plan was that we would be taken over the Hungarian border, from where my brother and I were to be delivered to my Aunt Rozsi and Uncle Kive who lived in the small town of Tolscva in the Tokaj region. My sister, then seven years old, was too young to join us. While my brother and I were quite ready to leave Slovakia, our companion was not. I remember the parting scene vividly. As we approached the border and were saying goodbye to our fathers, he refused to let go of his and to come with us. In great agitation his father, who was eager for us to leave under cover of darkness, slapped him and pushed him away. That was the last contact between father and son. The son probably died in a concentration camp some time between the summer of 1944 and the spring of 1945, during the

27

deportations of Hungarian Jews. His parents were deported from Slovakia – probably also in 1944. His mother and siblings died in the camps, but his father returned. It was very painful to see him after the war – my brother and I knew that we were constant reminders of the circumstances under which he and his thirteen-year-old son had parted.

From the vantage point of Jews in Slovakia, Hungary appeared to be a relatively safe place in the winter of 1942. Although early in the war years the Hungarian Parliament had enacted a series of anti-Jewish edicts, and several thousand 'stateless' Jews within its new borders were deported in 1941, the co-operation of the Hungarian Government with its Axis allies was less than wholehearted. The economic, social, political and communal lives of the Jews of Hungary were significantly disrupted, but for the first few years there were no roundups to work camps or deportations to concentration camps.

It was not until March 1944, when Hitler, dismayed at the 'lax' anti-Jewish policies of the Horthy government and frustrated by the lack of zeal of the Hungarian Army on the Russian front, ordered the occupation of Hungary, and the persecution of Jews became systematic and relentless. The Nazis and their German collaborators were keen to make up for lost time. Almost immediately after the occupation of Hungary, the Jews were required to wear the Star of David – which separated them from other citizens and marked them as legitimate targets for abuse by the local fascist militia. A few weeks later, all Jews were uprooted from their homes and crowded into a number of ghettos that were created both in the provinces and in Budapest. Getting a late start, and being surrounded by Russian troops, did not deter the Germans or their Hungarian allies from executing their ruthless deportation policies. Their efficiency, and their determination, was staggering. Three months after the German occupation of Hungary, 437,000 Jews had been deported to Auschwitz. Seventy per cent of Hungarian Jews were annihilated in the war. But, because deportations started toward the end of the war, when the Russians were poised at the Hungarian borders, a relatively high proportion of Hungarian Jews escaped deportation. Among them were about 50,000 individuals who were classified as Jews under the Nuremberg Laws because they had two or more Jewish grandparents, but who did not self-identify as Jews and had Christian spouses.

Although saddened by our departure, my parents were much relieved that at least two of their three children had succeeded in 'crossing to safety'. Disaster struck as soon as we crossed the border. Probably betrayed by an informer from Prešov, my brother, our companion and I (but not the guide, who left us soon after we entered Hungary – pointing us roughly in the direction toward the town of Košice) were apprehended by the Hungarian police and charged with illegal entry. For once, the charge against us was legitimate. Exhausted and frightened, we were interrogated for several hours at the local police station, one at a time. We knew that the three of us were being held in the same building, but we did not see each other and had no way of communicating.

I have three vivid memories of that day. The first one is of my response to the demand by the interrogators that I describe the person who helped us cross the border. Our guide was a burly man in his late twenties, but for reasons that are not clear to me, I described him as a small, dark, middle aged man. It was a deliberate lie without practical benefits. An accurate description would hardly have aided the police in capturing him, even had they been interested in doing so. By the time they obtained the information from me and could possibly have acted on it, he would have long since been back in his native village, indistinguishable from other young men who lived there. He was unlikely to attempt ever again to smuggle someone across the border at this particular crossing point. So why did I, a twelve-year-old, frightened child, take such a keen pleasure in deceiving my interrogators? Did I on some level recognize the liberty retained by a prisoner, articulated in so many war narratives, not to respond to the captors' demands – sometimes by telling an outright lie, at other times by refusing to answer the question? It is also possible that I was still too young to understand the seriousness of the situation. Maybe, as a strategy for survival, I pretended that it was all a game and I was at liberty to trick my opponent.

The second memory is that of being asked by one of the policemen why I shouted my answers. I made up the response on the spot, even if it was a non sequitur, claiming that because

I did not speak Hungarian well, I had to shout to be understood. I discovered years later, when I arrived in America and struggled to learn English, that people would speak to me in a loud voice, as often as not in baby talk, believing that they were helping me to understand them better! Maybe that was just punishment for the fib I had told a Hungarian representative of law and order. In truth, I shouted because I wanted my brother to hear the story I made up – that our parents had been deported from Slovakia and that we came to Hungary in search of relatives.

My third memory – and it is my last one of our young companion – is still painful. When asked whether he knew where he was he answered, truthfully, 'Košice'. His mistake was that he identified the town by its Slovak name rather than by its Hungarian designation, Kassa. He was yelled at and slapped hard. No one was ready to make allowance for a child whose vocabulary could not keep up with the rapid changes in European geography.

Our misfortune had a silver lining. Perhaps because we claimed to have no parents we were sent to the Jewish orphans' home in Košice instead of being taken back to the border and forced to return to Slovakia. My brother and our companion were placed in the boys' unit while I went to the girls' section, some distance away. Neither our father, nor our Hungarian relatives, could help us immediately, although I believe they knew where we were.

Life in the orphanage was austere but not cruel. What I found most difficult was the separation from my brother, who had become my only anchor in a world that was foreign and unwelcoming. Although we saw each other occasionally, we had to deal with our daily hardships without the comfort of each other's company. On some afternoons we were allowed to meet, but we spent most of the days and all of the nights in separate dormitories. From time to time we were visited by local Jews who showed an interest in us and brought us food to supplement our meagre meals.

Much as my brother and I missed each other, we had our first quarrel the day we were reunited at the Košice police station about six weeks after we had left it. The cause of the fight was a piece of salami! A few days before we were removed from the orphanages, my brother, with great ceremony and with a heavy

30

other-guarded

heart, shared with me half of a salami he had received from a benevolent visitor to his orphanage. Given the scarcity of any food, and especially of food that was as tasty and as nourishing as a piece of sausage, my brother was understandably annoyed that, when I was picked up by the police and, without explanation, ordered to pack my belongings, I forgot the salami, which I kept in the drawer next to my bed. Was that not my most precious possession? He determined right then and there, as he did on a few subsequent occasions, that I had neither the natural instincts nor the wit or requisite skills to survive the war, and that he would have to take care of me.

Another night in the now familiar police station. This time, our roommate was a young Gypsy, who tried to persuade us to escape from our ground floor cell by jumping out of the window when the guards were not paying attention. It was clear that for him, being in jail was just a fact of life, and running away was a tried and true strategy that had worked well in the past. My brother and I declined, primarily because we had nowhere to go. Maybe the Gypsies would have sheltered us for a while – but these were times when being a Gypsy was not much better than being a Jew. We may also have been discouraged from joining him by the many tales we had heard about Gypsies snatching children and turning them into young fortune-tellers. When morning came, we were once again asked to pack our belongings. My brother was clutching his half of the salami and looked reproachfully at me. Ignorant of our destination, we found out, after boarding a train, that we were headed for Ricse – a camp for political prisoners and Jewish refugees.

I do not know why we were taken out of the orphanage, why we landed in this particular camp, or why, after a few weeks, we were released into the care of our aunt and uncle. It may again have been through the intercession of my aunt's Hungarian officer friend, but I am not sure. If we were ever given an explanation, I do not remember it. Nor do I particularly care to know it now. To us it seemed that our fates were being determined haphazardly and without planning or purpose, most often by malevolent forces. We were too insignificant to deserve individual attention in a world that had been stood on its head, and yet things were happening to us. I do remember, however, that my brother and I were the only children in the camp. I was housed

or? after?

with the women and my brother with the men. We could cross from one section to another easily, and we were used as couriers for notes from husbands to wives and from young women to their boyfriends. I would like to believe that I did not read them, but I cannot be sure.

Ricse was a relatively short distance from Košice, perhaps 50 kilometres, but it involved a train change in Sátoraljaújhely. For me the ride was filled with adventure and memories of holidays, visits to grandparents, vacations, freedom. In my mind I heard the song we sang when we played in our courtyard in Prešov. It was like the English 'ring-a-ring-a-roses', with the lyrics *Wir fahren nach Amerika und wer fährt mit, auch du mein süsses Evalein* (any name could be substituted), *auch du kommst mit*. Yet I knew we were not going in the right direction to reach America – the promised land of milk and honey. Perhaps the English ending, 'ashes, ashes, we all fall down' would have been more appropriate.

The guard to whose care we were entrusted was kind. In an unforgettable gesture, at one station stop he leaned out of the window and bought us each an orange. One of the bright memories of that period is the smile on his face when he handed us the beautiful, and to us unavailable, fruit. Did he have children? Did he feel sorry for us? Did he know what awaited us? Kindness was unexpected and it confounded us. We were sad to part with him when, late that evening, he handed us over to a local police officer in Sátoraljaújhely, under whose supervision we spent the night before setting out for our final destination the following morning. I may have expected a reassuring pat on my head, or perhaps a conspiratorial wink from him, but that did not happen. Instead, in the presence of another policeman, our gentle guard became gruff and distant. He may have been reluctant to reveal his compassion and his humanity in front of a fellow police officer.

My brother and I shared a cell with a woman who had just been released from Ricse. When she heard where we were going she started to wail and then proceeded to describe, in great detail, the terrible conditions in the camp. This was not a good bedtime story, but when she ended her tale with the remark '*a hust leete'k rolam*' ('they ate the flesh off me'), my brother and I could not suppress our laughter. She must have weighed, even

32

in her emaciated state, well over 100 kilos, and the idea that she believed herself now to be skeletal provided comic relief. Nevertheless, we did not sleep well that night.

Conditions at Ricse were harsh – with hunger and bed bugs our constant companions. Occasionally the local police would come through the barracks and select the people who were to be sent to work camps. One day it was almost my turn. Three soldiers came to our section and picked out the people to be removed. I was one of them. Then I heard one of the soldiers whisper to the other, 'I cannot take this one, she has such sad eyes!' And so, having touched momentarily the heart of a man who undoubtedly was hardened to much human suffering, I was temporarily saved. From that time on I was referred to by the others in our dormitory, half affectionately and half mockingly, as the 'child with the sad eyes'. Ironically, having sad eyes could be very dangerous. Not infrequently, Jews who were living on assumed identities and looked Aryan – tall, blond and blue eyed – who were acculturated into the mainstream of society, and who spoke the language of the country in which they lived without any trace of an accent, were given away by the sad and hunted look in their eyes.

The first day of April 1943 will forever be etched in my memory as the day our Uncle Kive, and his daughter, Alice, appeared at the camp, ready to take us to their home in Tolcsva. When my brother came running with the great news and asked me to get ready to leave, I mocked him, saying that he could not play an April Fool's day joke on me! (I wonder how I knew the date, since every day was like April Fool's day.) Only after he accused me yet again of lacking the necessary instincts to get out of this war alive, which he followed by a threat to leave without me, did I finally relent. Happy as I was at the prospect of freedom, I was heartbroken to have to say goodbye to Magda, a young woman about twenty years old, who had been my bunk mate. She taught me some of the survival skills my brother thought were essential, and she helped me fight bed bugs, hunger, loneliness and fear. She was later deported to a concentration camp but survived the war. When I visited her in her home in 1946 neither she, nor I, could recapture the relationship we had forged in the camp. She was preoccupied with her upcoming marriage and I was dealing with adolescence.

Perhaps our inability to rekindle the intimacy of the camp was a healthy sign that both of us were beginning to live more normal lives, coupled with a reluctance to dwell on the past.

Once we walked out of the gates of the camp, it took two trains, and a few hours, to travel the roughly 40 kilometres from Ricse to Tolcsva, a small town in the Tokay region, where Uncle Kive served as rabbi to a community of 300 Jews. My brother and I became part of an extended family that included my aunt and uncle and their three children, Alice, Ocsi and Marica, all about the same age as we were, as well as my Aunt Ancsi who had arrived from Prešov before us, and my paternal grandmother. Only three of us survived the war: Alice, my brother and I.

We lived a quiet and uneventful life. My brother and I occasionally attended the local school; we milked cows, helped to make prune jam and learned to force feed geese. We also reported to the police once every two weeks, as we were required to do. We did not hear from our parents and knew little about their condition, although at one point my father succeeded in sending some money to help my uncle in his strained financial situation. The salary of a small town rabbi was barely adequate to feed four adults and five young people with healthy appetites. We were loved and we loved in return.

Shortly after the German occupation of Hungary in March 1944, all the Jews of Tolcsva were taken to a ghetto in Sátoraljaújhely, the provincial town in the Tokaj region which, only a little over a year earlier, had served as a stopover on our way from Košice to the camp in Ricse. We were frightened and disoriented. With infinite dignity and calm, my uncle, who had no illusions about the fate that awaited us, comforted his family and his congregation. As we were being interrogated, stripped of all our possessions and herded into close quarters, my uncle asked one of the Hungarian soldiers whether he could keep his watch. 'You will have no need of it', came the reply, 'because where you are going there will be a very big clock that will tell you your final hour'. 'But maybe the clockmaker did not set it right', my uncle countered. I feared he would be shot on the spot, but perhaps the guards did not hear him or were too busy preparing us for our final hour.

Returns 45 yrs later

This episode came back to me, with great vividness and intensity, in July 1993, when I returned to Košice after a 45-year absence. Walking deep in thought through the town, I noticed that no two clocks on the various public buildings and churches told the same time, as if God (or Einstein, or Kafka) were playing some trick on the inhabitants. Is there a right time, I wondered, and who measures it? And then, in a stream of consciousness that defies chronology and logic, I remembered two other episodes involving watches. The first one occurred in the Sátoraljaújhely ghetto, the second after the war.

time question

When we arrived at the ghetto my brother had one treasure left – a watch he had received for his Bar Mitzvah in June 1942, a few months before we left for Hungary – and he was determined not to part with it. The celebration of his Bar Mitzvah, a rite of initiation by which a young male takes on the responsibilities and burdens of the Jewish community, must have had special poignancy at a time when hundreds of Jews were being deported to concentration camps daily. I cannot even imagine the risks that he, so proud of his survival skills, must have taken to get that watch past the guards. The woodpile we found in the cellar of the house we shared with hundreds of other people, who were mostly strangers to us, provided a good hiding place for it. Whenever we could we crept into the cellar to check that it was still there – though we never pulled it out to see if it was ticking! I suspect that we endowed the watch with magical qualities that guaranteed that, as long as it was where we had hidden it, we too were safe. Alas, the watch did not make it out of the ghetto.

The second episode took place in October 1948, on a train ride from Prague to Naples, where my mother and her three children were to board the Vulcania and sail to America. Once again, we had to leave our possessions behind. We managed to salvage very little – a few trinkets, a gold bracelet and a watch. I do not remember what we did with the bracelet, which I still have, but I do remember that we hid the watch in the upholstered overhead straps in our sleeping bunks. We were frisked at the border, our bunks were searched, but no one thought to examine the somewhat tattered woollen straps, and the watch made it safely to America. Many years later my mother, who wore it every day, must have lost it. One morning she looked for it in its usual place, but it was not there.

Did the clockmaker make a mistake? While the ghettos in Poland lasted for several years, although with diminishing populations, the Hungarian ones were liquidated in a very short time. The end of the war seemed to be too close and the risk of delay too great, if the aim was to ensure that there would be no survivors. Between mid-May and July 1944, most of the roughly 500,000 Jews gathered in the ghettos were deported to Auschwitz.

My father must have known that the Hungarian ghettos were only very temporary way stations to concentration camps. He made several desperate attempts to get all of us out, only to be disappointed at the last moment. My sister remembers the Friday night when several peasants from neighbouring villages came to my parents' apartment in Prešov and took a letter from my father, undoubtedly with money in it, addressed to the same Hungarian police official, the acquaintance of his sister, Ancsi, who may have intervened on our behalf before, begging him to take us out of the ghetto. That Saturday, she recalls, my father stayed in bed and cried. Both events were so unusual that they remained deeply imprinted in her memory. At a time when so much sorrow went unanswered, it is unseemly even to conjecture that a father's tears could have saved his children. But, five days before the start of the deportations from the ghetto, a policeman appeared in our quarters with fake orders to take my brother and me to headquarters for interrogation, claiming that there was evidence that we had been used as couriers for the Hungarian Underground. The ploy worked for us, but it was too late to save the rest of my father's family. Once the deportations started, the Germans were in total control and there was no exit. My brother and I left the ghetto on a cold, rainy Saturday night in May 1944. When the gates closed behind us we could not have known that, with one exception, we would never see any of our relatives again. For us, the gates opened to temporary freedom; to them, a few days later, they opened to hell.

Crossing the border was difficult. The terrain was uneven, filled with wet leaves and prickly shrubs. To make matters worse, I had a very high temperature, which, ironically, may have saved me from more serious molestation by our crossing guard. When, finally, my brother and I were reunited with our parents and sister, there was relief, but no joy. We were heartsick

36

about those we left behind. When my father picked us up at the Prešov police station midday on Sunday, he was undoubtedly startled by our emaciated and unkempt appearance. But far more painful than our dishevelled looks must have been the anguish he heard in my brother's voice who, without an embrace or word of greeting, pleaded with my father to save the family we left behind. I can still hear his voice, 'You must save Uncle Kive'. I do not remember my father's response, but he knew it was too late. At the moment my brother still hoped that they could be saved, my father must have known that he had to stand by helplessly as his mother, two sisters, a brother-in-law and two nieces and a nephew were about to be transported out of the ghetto. In a world that was as chaotic and senseless as ours was at that time, perhaps it did not make sense to brood about justice and fairness. But we could not fail to ask, over and over again, then and later, why did we escape and they did not? Were we assigned a guardian angel, while they were abandoned to their fate? Why were we able to leave at the last possible minute and they remained trapped?

We mourned deeply for our Hungarian family, but it was only after the war that we found out their fate. Upon arrival in Auschwitz, my grandmother and Aunt Ancsi, who had a club-foot, were immediately marked for annihilation. Aunt Rozsi, Alice and Marica were sent to the Plazsow labour camp near Cracow, where, since 1943, Schindler operated the factory for his 1,000 Jews. As the Russian Army approached Cracow, Plaszow was evacuated and Rozsi, Alice and Marica were sent back to Auschwitz. In September 1944, Alice was separated from her mother and sister, and never saw them again. Now it was a race between the Russian Army and the angel of death. When the inmates of Auschwitz were evacuated, Alice was sent to a work camp near Leipzig, and when that city came under siege, she, together with thousands of others, was forced to go on the 23-day death march to Theresienstadt. She was liberated on 9 May 1945. Uncle Kive survived until a few weeks before liberation. He was shot in the Flossenburg camp in March 1945. The fate of my cousin, Ocsi, is unclear. After the war, we heard a rumour that he had survived the war and been captured by the Russians. But the story was never substantiated and our efforts, and those of his sister, Alice, to find him, or at least someone who had seen him after the liberation, were unsuccessful. <u>Did he die in a concentration camp or in a gulag?</u>

I have often wondered about the fate of another member of our Tolcsva community, a young man considered by adults and children alike 'the village idiot'. His name, I think, was Laci. At what seemed to be pre-appointed times, he appeared at the gate of our little garden to receive food and engage in conversation. He did not speak much, but listened attentively, seeming to enjoy in equal measure the food and the human interaction. I remember being both curious and uneasy about him, and though he was friendly and harmless, I went to some length not to be in the garden during his visits. I am quite certain that he was deported from Tolcsva, although I do not remember him in our transport to the ghetto, nor can I recall his presence once we arrived there. He was not the sort of person one would notice in a crowd. The surprising news about him came after the war. From the accounts of eyewitnesses we learned that when he arrived in the concentration camp he underwent a sudden and miraculous personal transformation. The timid half-wit became, under the Nazi whip, a capable, helpful, resourceful and courageous person concerned not for his own survival, but for the survival of others. I do not begin to understand the psychological forces behind this metamorphosis and I can only wonder whether he himself, during the short period he lived in the camp, was aware of the profound changes in his being. Had he survived the war and come back to his native village, would he have remained the person he had become for a brief moment, or would he have reverted to his old self? What <u>internal</u> forces were unleashed by unmitigated evil that could not be touched by kindness?

****

I do not know much about my parents' life in Slovakia during the year and a half we spent in Hungary (winter 1942 to spring 1944). From what I have been able to piece together from my sister's fragmented memories, periods of relative calm were followed by periods of ruthless persecutions. Calm meant the ability to survive under the conditions prescribed by the Nazis –

severe restrictions of movement, constant harassment, life reduced to survival at the most basic level. Yet, the family seemed to have had enough food, because my sister remembers how badly they all felt when, while eating their Saturday meal, they received a letter from my brother and me, probably written from the orphanage in Košice, reporting that we had just had breakfast of some black bread and coffee. But normalcy was only an illusion and a charade in the small Jewish community of Prešov, easily interrupted by harsh decrees, individual violence and collective persecutions. Thus, it was normal that my mother and sister would go to a local bakery and get a sweet and coffee in the afternoon; it was also normal that one day, without warning, they were confronted with the sign 'Jews and dogs not allowed'. With the stroke of a pen they were deprived of their sweets, and of any illusions they may still have had.

As head of the ÚŽ, my father may have had, from time to time, some advance knowledge about important, upcoming events. He used whatever protection his official position offered him to help not only the remaining members of his community by warning them of new edicts or roundups, but also the small trickle of Jews who had managed to escape from labour camps and from the ghettos of Poland to Slovakia on their way, by underground railroad, to Hungary. Our house became the refuge of some eminent rabbis who needed temporary shelter. Among them, I believe, were the Verboer rebbe and his wife, as well as a descendent of the Bobover rebbe and his family. My sister remembers a fourteen year old boy who, standing in our kitchen, dissolved in tears when he saw my mother discarding potato peels. What she carelessly threw into the garbage could have made the difference between life and death to the friends in the ghetto he had just left behind. She also remembers the sheer terror of another child who stayed with them. When he refused to pay attention to my mother's admonition to keep quiet, she, out of old habit, threatened to 'call the policeman'. In the past, the policeman was the symbol of external, but relatively benign, authority. Within his own short lifetime, the police were not the guardians of law and order, but killers of the unprotected.

The presence of refugees and the existence of the underground railroad could hardly have escaped the watchful eyes of

39

the Germans and their Slovak collaborators. Bribes, ransom and the exchange of other goods must have been arranged by the Bratislava Working Group and, perhaps, by some members of international organizations. It was an effort on a modest scale, and of limited success. Many who escaped from Poland were later caught and killed in Hungary. These rescue activities were double edged. On the one hand, the ability to provide a temporary safe haven for the refugees must have given the remaining Jews of Prešov some comfort. On the other hand, the tales the refugees told about the hells from which they had escaped left little doubt about the nature and extent of the German Final Solution. Although many had fled from the so-called work camps and not from the death camps, they bore witness to conditions that were harsh and cruel beyond most people's imagination. The seemingly inexhaustible supply of slave labour from the occupied territories, including large parts of the Soviet Union, provided little economic incentive, either to the government, or to the industrial employers, for preserving the lives or health of their slaves. Replacements were free, and the relentless decimation of the ranks helped to accomplish the aims of the Final Solution. Slave labourers were disposable objects.

Then, in the summer of 1943, the Germans and their Slovak allies started another round of deportations and demanded ransom as a condition for stopping them. They were torn between two conflicting desires – to secure funds for their increasingly hopeless prosecution of the war, and to complete the elimination of all Jews from the face of the countries they occupied. Avarice won, and when the full ransom was delivered, the deportations stopped.

On the day of our return from the Sátoraljaújhely ghetto in May 1944, our family situation was precarious, and our fate uncertain. Our arrival coincided with the deadline for all remaining Jews in eastern Slovakia to move to points further west. The Russian Army was poised on the eastern border and the Slovak Government wanted all Jews removed from the 'threatened' territories. One can only guess at the reasons for the decree. It is possible that final deportations initiated from a less beleaguered part of Slovakia were deemed to be simpler than trying to secure transport trains so close to the front lines. It is

equally possible that in their last frantic attempts to boost their
war machinery, the Germans once again hoped to ransom the
remaining Jews for guns and trucks, as they had done in the
past and as Eichmann and his deputy, Dieter Wisličeny, tried to
do again when the Jews of Budapest were being rounded up for
deportation. All we understood was that we had no choice and
that we had to uproot.

On 15 May 1944, we boarded one of the last trains taking
Jews from Prešov to the more western parts of the country. Our
assigned destination was Nitra, a mid-sized city in the south-
western part of Slovakia. What we left behind were our remaining possessions, our decimated communal life and whatever
hope we had retained that no matter how difficult our situation
might be, it would not get worse and we would survive the war.
We moved into a tiny apartment in the Jewish Quarter, on
Palánok 5, next to my mother's Aunt Ida and Uncle David and
their two children – Greta, who was a few years older than I,
and Immy, who was about my sister's age. They had been
forced to move to Nitra in 1941, when a number of Jews from
Bratislava, the capital of Slovakia, were relocated to smaller
towns and assigned to work essentially as slave labourers. They
were still in deep mourning for their oldest son, Arthur, who
had been deported in 1942. For the next four months we saw
each other daily and derived some comfort from our extended
family life.

The story of our family reunion in May 1944 began with the
parting from my father's relatives in the Sátoraljaújhely ghetto.
The story of our move into hiding five months later begins with
another final parting, this time from my mother's aunt and
uncle and from cousin Immy. None of them survived the war.
(Greta came into hiding with us.)

In October 1944, all the remaining Jews of Nitra were rounded up. Uncle David, Aunt Ida and Immy were discovered hun-
kering in the attic. Uncle David was summarily shot, and Immy
and his mother were deported. After the war, when we searched
for relatives, we heard rumours that she had survived, but we
never saw her again. Perhaps she became one of the nameless
victims who died during the long trek back home – of typhus, of
starvation, of despair. One of the most haunting images I retain
is that of Immy, a most beautiful child, sitting in the courtyard

playing the harmonica. In my mind, he stands for hundreds and thousands of young boys who never had a chance to become adults.

Our last eight months in Nitra were spent with the woman and her daughter to whom we owe our lives. This book is mostly about them. Everything else is a prelude to their story.

Salvation

4 Mária Krescanková

On 3 July 1997, at a ceremony at Yad Vashem, the title 'Righteous Among the Nations' was officially conferred on Mária Göblová Krescanková, and her daughter, Vlastimila (Vlasta) Krescanková. Of the eight people who had shared a common space and a common fate during the last eight months of the war, four were present: my brother, my sister, Vlasta and I. The absence of our parents and of Mária were powerful reminders of the 52 years that had elapsed since the liberation of Slovakia, and stood as a reproach to us for not having acted sooner. In the stillness of the warm and cloudless summer day, with gentle breezes blowing from the Judaean Hills, I imagined that I heard softly whispered reproaches: 'Why did you wait so long?' My father died in Israel in 1970 and Mária died in Slovakia in 1982. My mother, at the age of 90, was too old to make the trip. And we had lost touch with our cousin, Greta, who, soon after the war, went to live with her paternal relatives in England. She married young and raised a large, very Orthodox family.

But there were also compensations for having waited. My brother's whole family – his wife Leah, and their three children, two of them with spouses – live in Israel and came to the ceremony, as did my daughter, who is an art teacher in Elizabeth, New Jersey. We were joined by my oldest and only childhood friend, Eva, my sister's close friend Bruria, a native Israeli, and Leah's sister-in-law, Shoshana, and her daughter Corinne. Altogether we were 15 people.

For all of us the day started early, as we travelled from the north and from the south to reach Yad Vashem, the Holocaust Memorial, nestled in the valley outside the city of Jerusalem. The distance for some of us was an hour's drive; for others it took two and a half or three hours by car or by public transportation. Although we set out from five different locations, fearing traffic jams and road blocks, each group allowed extra

43

travel time. As if by pre-arrangement, all of us arrived at ten o'clock, an hour before the start of the ceremony. We were glad of the extra time to walk around, to think and to remember. Vlasta and I talked about her mother, trying to make her an active participant in the ceremony honouring her.

The two parts of the ceremony took place in two startlingly different locations and lasted a little over an hour. It began in the *Ohel Yiskor* (Tent of Remembrance), a stark but peaceful stone structure. The dark and empty space is illuminated only by the flame from the 'eternal light'. The locations of the 22 major concentration camps are engraved on the floor, and each contains ashes brought back from the 'killing fields'. A cantor recited *Kaddish,* the prayer of remembrance of the dead. *Kaddish* is also an affirmation of the sanctity of life and of the divine presence in it, and a rededication of those present to the community of the deceased. It is also a prayer for universal peace and justice. Vlasta was invited to turn up the switch on the 'eternal flame" in order to create a burst of light. That was the religious part of the ceremony. Vlasta thus had a central role in an ancient Jewish ritual. It was conducted with much dignity and grace, expressing a specific tradition with a universal message. Deeply moved, I thought – for a brief moment – that it might be possible to reconcile radical evil with divine justice.

In contrast to the starkness of the Hall of Remembrance, the second part of the ceremony was held in the 'Garden of the Righteous Among the Nations'. A serene grove which comes into view at the end of a long avenue of trees with commemorative plaques bearing the names of those who risked their lives to save a Jew, it is green and lush, richly planted with bushes, shrubs and flowers. It speaks of rebirth and regeneration and reminds us of our oneness with nature. One side of the grove is bound by a stone wall with panels, arranged first by country and then by city, bearing the names of those individuals who had been recognized by Yad Vashem. In the section blocked out for Slovakia, Vlasta saw the two spaces reserved for her and her mother in the city of Prešov. In the winter of 1998 my nephew, who lives in America, visited Yad Vashem and reported that their names had already been inscribed on the 'Wall of the Righteous'. Their deeds are now carved in stone.

44

Three speakers participated in this part of the ceremony. The director of the Division of the Righteous, who told the story, in English and in Hebrew, of what Mária and Vlasta had done; the director of Yad Vashem, who put their individual deeds into the context of the relatively small group of people who had participated in the rescue of Jews; and a retired judge of the Supreme Court of Israel, who headed the commission that reviewed our petition to have Mária and Vlasta inscribed in Yad Vashem. The most moving part for me was Vlasta's response, delivered in halting English. She thanked Yad Vashem for the honour bestowed on her and her mother and expressed the hope that the events we were commemorating would never be repeated again. The ceremony ended with the presentation of a large bouquet of spring flowers, a medal inscribed with the names of both Mária and Vlasta, and a framed Certificate of Honour awarded to Mária Göblová Krescanková and her daughter, Vlasta Krescanková. One side of the specially designed medal bears the talmudic inscription, in Hebrew and in French, which translated reads, 'he who saves a single life is as though he has saved the whole world', and also the words, 'With thanks from the people of Israel'. The other side of the medal tells the story symbolically: many hands grasping at a rope of barbed wire encircling the globe. While the ceremony was intensely personal, honouring two exceptional individuals, it also embraced the victims who perished, all those who were saved, and all the righteous women and men who risked their lives to save them.

At the time of the ceremony, more than 13,000 individuals had been recognized as 'Righteous Among the Nations,' representing over 5,000 authenticated rescue stories. Some ceremonies had taken place in Israel, others in Israeli diplomatic offices in the home country of the rescuer. To us, Israel seemed the right place to bestow the honour on Mária and Vlasta Krescanková. At Yad Vashem we were joined not only by friends and relatives, but by a grateful nation. Radio, newspapers and television covered the ceremony. It was both familial and communal.

As we stood silently listening to the speakers, we thought not only of the dead, but also of the new generation of children and grandchildren, both present and absent, who owe their existence to the courage and compassion of Mária Krescanková. For us of the older generation, the occasion was an opportunity to acknowledge publicly our debt to Mária and Vlasta. It also provided a sense of closure to a very important and painful chapter in our lives and the lives of our parents. For our children, the retelling of the rescue story created a connection to events which for them had only a historical reality. I was deeply moved when my niece, Rivka, told me how much it meant to her to experience, in real time, a piece of the past about which her father had remained largely silent. My own daughter, who knows bits and pieces about the war years, gained a new understanding of the effect that those years may have had on my childhood, and more permanently throughout my life. It is natural to want to protect our children from knowing too much about the traumas of our past. We fear that by sharing our experiences we may kill their optimism, their joy in life, their confidence that the world is a hospitable place and above all, that we can and will protect them from evil. If there were times within our own memories when parents could not protect their children, can we protect them? Yet there is a price to be paid for the silence. Children 'read' their parents' past in actions which they cannot understand and for which they have no context. My daughter never understood why I mourned so deeply on Yom Kippur – not for my sins (though I may have many) – but for those who could fast even when there was so little to eat and who, even in the most extreme situations, could still recite Kol Nidre and pray to a God who had abandoned them. At Yad Vashem we did not have to tell stories. The past was present – our family and Vlasta witnesses to events that happened more than 50 years earlier, acts that saved our lives and which, in different fragments, entered the lives of all of us.

For Vlasta, who continues to live in a country where acts of rescue are regarded largely with disdain, if not outright hostility, the love, gratitude and affection of all those who were present at Yad Vashem affirmed the historical significance of the deeds she and her mother had performed at mortal risk to themselves. And for all of us, Mária Krescanková was not a ghost out of the past, but an immediate and wonderful presence. She would have liked the ceremony, although she would probably have found it incomprehensible that it was held in her honour, and would have done her best to deflect attention from herself to those who were saved.

****

I last saw Mária Krescanková (I will refer to her as 'Teta', Slovak for 'aunt', since that is what we called her) on a cold October morning in 1948 when my mother, a German citizen under the United States immigration laws (she came originally from Hamburg), and my brother, sister and I set out for America. My father, a Czechoslovak national, was not granted a visa to the United States. He left for Israel in the spring of 1949, when the situation for the Jews of Czechoslovakia became precarious once again. When we said goodbye, I could not have imagined that I would never hug Teta again; that Vlasta and I would be in advanced middle age before we saw each other again; that my father would not join us in America. Nor, for that matter, could I have expected that we would set foot in New York on the night Harry Truman, against great odds, was elected President.

From the beginning, I kept in touch with Teta. I wrote to her each Christmas and as soon as I had a job I sent her modest sums of money. We wrote to each other about the small things in our lives and about our marriages, our work and our children. I believe she was proud of me. I know she loved me. Her story is not only about her heroism, but also about her love. I think she knew how attached I was to her, although I failed to give her the one gift she would have most wanted – a reunion. She was reunited with us at Yad Vashem, in our tributes, our memories and our hearts.

Mária Göblová Krescanková, the only child of Albert and Helena Krescanko, was born on 2 January 1915. Having lost both her parents at a young age, she was entrusted to the care of her grandparents, with whom I believe she did not have a particularly close relationship. At fourteen, eager to strike out on her own, she left both her school and her grandparents' house and moved to Prešov to find work and to live by herself. Her daughter, Vlasta, was born in December 1933, a few days short of Teta's nineteenth birthday. It is perhaps not surprising that a woman who did not receive much love and nurturing in her youth would develop, early on, a sense of independence and a confidence in her ability to chart her own course. Never a conformist, Teta's moral code was not built on religious faith, political commitments or social approbation. Hers came from an internal command. What is more surprising is that out of her sense of marginality she developed a great capacity for love and a sense of unswerving loyalty to the people who put their trust in her.

Teta's first job was as a clerk at the municipal coal mine. Her second job was as a cashier at the *mikvah*, the Jewish public and ritual bath. Even as a young woman, she felt comfortable in an Orthodox Jewish environment, and she continued her work there after the outbreak of overt and virulent anti-Semitism. From 1939 on she must have been harassed, threatened and mocked for her association with the Jewish community. Why did she stay on? In a war-time economy she could surely have found a less demanding, and – from the point of view of her neighbours – a less demeaning way to earn a living. Her entitlement to employment in the war economy would have been bolstered by the claim that she was no longer willing to work for Jews. Her decision to seek other employment would have been understood, applauded and rewarded. But she refused to give in to social pressures to distance herself from the Jewish community.

The first time we called on Teta for help was in the spring of 1944, when the Slovak Government, after months of relative quiet and without any advance warning, though undoubtedly in consultation with Berlin, ordered the deportation of all the remaining Jews of Prešov. Over the years, many of the edicts against the Jews came suddenly and were put into effect immediately. This strategy accomplished two things: it caught the victims unaware and unprepared and, perhaps even more important, it was a terrifying and concrete manifestation of the absolute power of the state and the helplessness of the intended victims. Without hope for a reprieve or a miracle, my father had no choice but to go into hiding. Pretending to be casual strollers on a warm weekday afternoon he and my mother, with my sister between them, but of course without the Star of David on their garments, headed for Teta's apartment. My brother and I were at this time still trapped in the Sátoraljaújhely ghetto. In her large and then quite fashionable pocketbook, my mother must have carried all the liquid assets we still possessed. My father's briefcase contained my sister's crumpled *shabbos* dress, which she was not allowed to wear for fear that it would call too much attention to a family out for a walk on a weekday afternoon. But my sister, then eight years old, refused to leave without it, and there was no time for negotiations. Whether through luck or miracle, they reached their destination. When, after a few days, the government, as a result of either political calculation, whim, or, most likely, a bribe from the Bratislava Working Group, reversed itself with the announcement that instead of being deported, the Jews could leave Prešov voluntarily and move further west, my parents left Teta's apartment and returned home. Hoping that my brother and I would be rescued from the Hungarian ghetto before they had to leave Prešov, they wanted to be in a place where we would find them if we returned.

As so often during the war years, moments of reprieve were also moments of great anguish and uncertainty. For Teta and Vlasta, this brief interlude of harbouring Jews could have meant instant death. Had our parents been followed to their destination, or had she been betrayed by one of her neighbours, the most likely outcome would have been a summary execution of the three adults and two children. The carefully drawn racial and legal boundaries between Jews and non-Jews disappeared instantaneously when Gentiles proffered a helping hand. Teta was well aware of the risks but neither then, nor at any other time, did she calculate the odds. Hers was a moral calculus, not a calculus of self-interest.

By the spring of 1944, the situation of the remaining Jews in Prešov was so precarious that my parents and Teta must have worked out several contingency plans in advance, each one built on the assumption that Teta would provide a hiding place for us, either in Prešov or in another part of Slovakia. In 1944, we could not hope to find strangers who would risk their lives to provide shelter for us in the event that we faced deportation or were forced to leave Prešov. Without knowing the precise time when all the remaining Jews would be deported from every town, village and hamlet, my parents tried to prepare for the next and perhaps final stage in our battle for survival. Fortunately for us, there was a short reprieve between the time my family sought refuge in Teta's apartment and the day we had to leave Prešov on 15 May 1944.

While our general strategy may have been worked out in advance, we had no road map for our move to Nitra. There was no time to plan our departure and we had to invent the move under extremely difficult circumstances. The evacuation order forcing the remaining Jews to move into the centre of the country came suddenly and was executed swiftly. Our survival now depended on Teta and on her ability to secure a place in a new town where she could establish a household that would also serve as our hiding place.

My family took the train to Nitra the day after my brother and I returned to Prešov from the ghetto, which was also the deadline for all the remaining Jews to leave the city and move further west. Teta and Vlasta came with us.

Although my family travelled in one compartment and Teta and Vlasta in another, once we boarded the train we were headed for a common destination and an uncommon danger. We had no choice, but Teta did. Voluntarily and without the expectation or promise of any remuneration, then or later (if there was to be a later), she packed her possessions, pulled up her roots, and embarked on a journey of unknown duration, filled with danger and uncertainty. She was brave to offer a temporary shelter to my family during an unexpected roundup of Jews. But it was a giant leap to go from there to uprooting herself and her child, leaving everything that was familiar and secure behind, riding a train into darkness. She could easily have hunkered down and stayed in Prešov until the end of the war. With the dissolution of the Jewish community she had lost her job, but not her place. That she gave up voluntarily.

In hindsight, our forced removal to the centre of the country was a blessing. In Prešov we were known, and Teta, under suspicion for having worked for the Jewish community, could have been easily betrayed by someone who knew her, or us. In Nitra we were strangers and no one recognized us or was looking for us. Hence, when a few months later the time came for my family to move from our temporary apartment on the Palánok in Nitra, which we had rented upon our arrival, and go into hiding, it was easier to vanish without a trace. My brother and I could assume new identities, buttressed by false birth certificates

1. Mária Krescanková, before her marriage, age 31 (1946).

2. Šalomon Reinitz, age 40 (1941).

3. Rachel Reinitz, age 36 (1943).

4. Eva Reinitz, age 9; Gabriela Reinitz, age 4; Alexander Reinitz, age 11 (1940).

5. Front: Aunt Rozsi and Uncle Kive Kornitzer. Rear, left to right: Alexander Reinitz; Aunt Ansci Reinitz; Alice, Ocsi and Marica Kornitzer; Eva Reinitz (1943 or 1944).

6. Schoolfriends Nuša and Eva (1948).

7. Eva and Eva (1948).

8. Mária Göblová Krescanková (1960s).

9. Robert Göblov and Mária Göblová Krescanková at the time of their marriage (1953).

10. Mária Góblová Krescanková; Robert Göblov; Vlasta Krescanková (1960s).

11. Vlasta Krescanková receiving Certificate of Honour, Yad Vashem, 3 July 1997.

our father had managed to obtain for us. My sister was too young to participate in our transformation. It takes a certain maturity and considerable cunning to maintain the fiction of a false persona – to both be, and not be, the person you appear to be. Teta and Vlasta retained their names but added new features to their biographies. Most important, no one in Nitra knew that Teta had worked for the Jewish community in Prešov – surely a black mark for a patriotic Slovak.

While our family lived at Palánok 5, the Jewish enclave in Nitra, Teta and Vlasta, who had their own temporary accommodations some distance from us, started their search for a secure hiding place. Undoubtedly, Teta was looking for a place where newcomers could blend in easily and where neighbours kept more or less to themselves. Since there were significant population movements toward the end of the war, she hoped our arrival would not be noteworthy. The first place they rented became unavailable just as they were ready to move in, which caused all of us considerable distress. Time was of the essence, and any delay could make the difference between life and death. In the end, they rented a small cottage on Čulenova ulica (Čulenova Street) in a working class neighbourhood, called Črmáň, which was connected by a bridge to the town of Nitra. It was a one room house with a sizeable kitchen, pantry, attic, and an outhouse in the garden. For six months it was a home to eight people, including our cousin Greta; four were in hiding and never ventured out; of the other four, two had original birth certificates and two had forged ones. Only after our liberation did we find out that the first house Teta had wanted to rent had been taken by seven young Jewish men. Whether they were in hiding, or living with false identities, I do not know. I do know that shortly before the end of the war they were either betrayed, or discovered, during a routine search, and shot on the spot.

Teta quickly took possession of the house. She used the time before our arrival to introduce herself to the neighbours and to tell her family story, which she constructed with great skill and imagination. And the story was credible. Since the Russian Army was close to the Slovak border, her husband, a policeman in the eastern part of Slovakia, insisted that she and Vlasta move to a safer place in the interior of the country. She was to be joined shortly by her young niece and nephew (i.e. my brother and me) who still lived in Prešov, so that they too would escape the invading army. Her husband stayed to fight for Tiso and for the future of the Slovak Republic. Her rhetoric was appropriately patriotic, with just the right tinge of anti-Semitism to earn her stripes with her neighbours.

When a few days later my brother and I, once again separated from our parents and sister, arrived on the Črmáň with our false birth certificates and new identities, we were expected and welcomed. I was transformed into Magda Kašprišinová and my brother became my cousin, Toni Kašprišin. Because we had false papers, we could move around with relative freedom. It was important for us to establish that a family of four lived in the house, which would, we hoped, make the addition of my parents and sister less noticeable when they arrived. Since they did not have false papers, they would never surface – but it would be easier to account for the noise level of the house if our neighbours, right from the beginning, were given the idea that there were four tenants in it. We wanted to be seen as a family unit escaping the invading enemy armies. Though our neighbours did not know it, there was, of course, an even more important reason why my brother and I moved in as early as possible. In the event that my parents and sister could not reach the house, at least my brother and I would be safe. As was the case for most families, my parents were willing to be separated from us if that gave us even the smallest chance of surviving the war.

My brother and I did not construct an elaborate genealogical tree with sets of Christian grandparents, aunts and uncles. We probably knew that if our identities were ever to be questioned, our false papers would not protect us even from the most superficial scrutiny. In any case, my brother, certified by his false birth certificate to have been born a Christian, was marked by the 'sign of the Covenant' on his body, one that Toni Kašprišin would not have carried. Although the papers provided only very limited safety, we carefully practised our names – Toni and Magda, Magda and Toni. During the nine months we lived on the Črmáň only once did I slip up and called my brother by his real name, 'Ali' (short for Alexander). He instinctively responded, and it was too late for me to backtrack. Without waiting for questions from the other children who looked puzzled, I mumbled something like – Oh, when he was smaller he was fat and I teased him by calling him Ali-Baba, which made him angry. I had no idea what the connection between a fat little boy and Ali-Baba might be. Perhaps once upon a time I had seen drawings in a book of Persian fairy tales. Fortunately, no one raised the question. Luck continued to be an essential ingredient in our day to day survival.

Our family of four settled in quickly. We tried to delay the arrival of my parents and sister as long as possible. Without the physical presence of the people who would be hiding in the house, Teta, Vlasta, my brother and I could move more freely in the neighbourhood and establish ourselves in it. It would also shorten the time that those who did not have new identities would have to be invisible. By minimizing the time they spent in hiding we increased the chance that all of us would be liberated before we were discovered. While the four of us felt accepted and relatively safe, we knew that the threshold of danger would increase significantly when everybody moved in. Once again, we were racing against time.

Teta's temperament was open and playful. She loved people and was a good storyteller. Although she would not have chosen the part that was thrust upon her, she played her role with remarkable skill and energy. She had a number of 'family' pictures on the mantle – most prominent among them a large photograph of her 'husband' in uniform – a handsome and trustworthy fellow to whom, people thought, I bore a striking resemblance. She was gutsy, matter of fact, the model of an honest, open and uncomplicated person. What she did not reveal was her immense courage, her ability to ward off suspicion, her fierce protective instincts and her talent for risk management. Under different circumstances she might have been an actress or a spy. Under all circumstances she would have been a person of extraordinary courage and moral commitment. For us she was Teta – the woman to whom we entrusted our lives.

The fate of the remaining Jews of Slovakia was sealed on 29 August 1944, when a group of partisans who had been active for two years in the eastern and central parts of Slovakia formally declared an uprising against the Slovak regime and its German allies. The uprising, spearheaded by officers in the Slovak army and supported financially and politically by the Czechoslovak Government in exile, was soon joined by a number of civilians, among them members of the communist underground and many young Jewish men and women who had escaped deportations by hiding in the countryside. At the height of the uprising, close to 16,000 soldiers and civilians, of whom roughly 10 per cent were Jews, fought fiercely against the forces loyal to Tiso and the SS units that joined them. The first few weeks brought much success. The partisans made substantial territorial gains, captured the town of Banská Bystrica in the centre of Slovakia, where they established their official headquarters. Their location allowed them to take control of important railway links to the eastern front. We were spellbound by their triumphs; fearful and jubilant at the same time. For a brief moment in September 1944, we allowed ourselves to hope that Nitra was our final way station to imminent liberation. But as so often happened during the war years, happiness rapidly turned into a sense of doom. By the end of October, barely two months after the start of the uprising, the German Army attacked the partisan units in full force and, with superior manpower and ammunition, speedily defeated them. Their revenge was swift and merciless, on Jews and non-Jews alike. Thousands of partisans were killed, among them the Jews who had risked leaving their hiding places to join in the war to liberate Slovakia. All the remaining Jews of Slovakia who did not join the uprising, about 9,000 in all, were now marked for deportation to Birkenau – the penultimate chapter of the Final Solution. The final chapter was written during the death marches forced on the inmates of concentration camps days, or even hours, before they were to be liberated.

I recall vividly the moment when, standing in the kitchen in our Črmáň house, I learned that the roundup of Jews in Nitra had started. A neighbour came in and reported, quite gleefully, that all the Jews were to gather on the town square, each with one suitcase, ready for the train ride that would carry them to oblivion. I wanted to run, to scream, to bang my fists against the counter, but I remained mute. Instead, I picked up an onion from the vegetable basket and, as if in a trance, I started to slice it. Tears were now rolling down my cheeks, caused by the onion in my hand, and not the dread in my heart. The neighbour continued chatting, but I did not hear her. To this day I remember the overwhelming sense of hopelessness and despair I felt at that moment. After all the separations from my parents and

sister this was the first time that I knew that they were in imminent danger and I was convinced that I would never see them
again. I wanted to take revenge on the messenger. The knife in
my hand could have been the murder weapon. Fortunately, I
must have picked up some of Teta's acting ability which I had
much admired, for, after the initial shock, my savage instincts
turned into sweet dissembling. Continuing to slice the onion I
was putting into the frying pan, I said, as nonchalantly as I
could, that I hate to cook onions because they always make my
eyes water. Then I quickly changed the subject from onions and
from deportations. My terror was real, but under control.

Once again, Teta and my father must have had some advance
warning before the Jews were to report to the town square, and
immediately went into action. Precisely at noon, when the
guards at the bridge connecting the Črmáň with the city of Nitra
were changing, my father and my sister, dressed carefully so as
not to attract attention, walked to our house. Blue eyed and
blond, my father could pass for a Slovak. My sister had dark curly
hair and might have attracted more attention. But she was a
nine-year-old child in the company of a respectable, Aryan-
looking gentleman. I do not remember how they got into the
house without being seen. In the evening, Teta returned to Nitra
to pick up my mother, who looked much more Jewish, intending
to smuggle her into the house under cover of darkness. In broad
daylight my mother, with her jet black hair and brown eyes,
could never have passed for a Gentile, especially not in a world
on the lookout for Jews making a last desperate attempt to escape
the dragnet of the SS and the local police. My mother, however,
refused to leave unless Teta agreed to take at least one of the two
children of her aunt, with whom we had lived on Palánok 5. The
aunt and her family had made a last minute plan to hide in the
attic of the house where they lived, although they must have
known that this would provide only a very temporary and very
unsafe shelter. My mother's young cousin, Immy, was circumcised and his older sister, Greta, then about fifteen, looked very
Jewish. Neither of them had false papers that might have ward-
ed off a superficial police check when they were crossing the
bridge to our house on the Črmáň. It is one thing for two women
wearing head scarves and pretending to be in deep conversation
to pass unnoticed; it is quite another thing for three women, one

still a child, to make the same crossing. And if they were caught on the way to our house, our cover would have been blown and all of us would have perished before we had a chance to put our plan into effect.

Teta now had a dilemma. Quite apart from the danger of getting two people safely into the house, the long term consequences were also serious. To hide another person presented grave risks to all of us, both by increasing the likelihood that we would be discovered and by obliging us to feed another person who did not have a ration card. Yet, not to accept my mother's condition would have exposed Greta and my mother to almost certain death. After what to us seemed hours of waiting, Teta returned to the Črmáň alone and explained why my mother did not come.

Underlying all our practical calculations was, once again, an excruciating moral dilemma. How do we weigh the claims of saving one additional life against the claims of seven others (including my mother) to create the safest possible conditions for survival? Was my mother's stand ethically justified, or was she creating irresponsible roadblocks in a moment of extreme crisis? On what basis do we choose between saving the brother or the sister? Why not both? What claim does any single individual have to being saved, while others, through no fault of their own, are being killed?

In the end, my father and Teta agreed that Greta could stay with us, but it was a hard decision, both on ethical and on practical grounds. In hindsight, it was perhaps easier for my parents, who themselves were at grave risk, to accept the additional risk of having another person stay with us than it would have been for Teta, who had not only put herself and her daughter at risk, but had also taken on the obligation to protect our family. But our luck held out, and Teta returned safely with Greta and my mother. We were now all together – three adults and five children; four ration cards and three beds; two people with their own birth certificates; two people with false birth certificates; and four people without any papers.

Despite these superficial distinctions, all of us belonged to an endangered species. We did not know how long we would be able to hold out or how long it would take to have our cover blown. With no certainties and no illusions, Teta became the head of our household.

5 Life in Hiding

My memories of our daily lives during the eight months we were in hiding are fragmented and episodic. This is especially true if by 'daily' we mean the ebb and flow of feelings and routines that punctuate any 24-hour period. It may be a lapse of memory, but it may also be that the need to stay alert and watchful at all times overshadowed them and, in retrospect, any rote performance of tasks. We did not have a routine. Hence, it is easier to recall the things we did not do than those we did. We did not attend school; we did not visit or entertain friends; we had no relatives who dropped by; we never gathered around a table to eat a meal or to play a game; we did not go on outings, and we did not distinguish weekdays from weekends. Perhaps my mother said prayers on Friday night and Saturday, but if she did, they were private.

Yet we must have developed strategies that allowed us to pass the daylight hours. Although we were a family of avid readers, I cannot think of a single book I read or that we discussed. We did not have books in our house – they would have been totally out of place in our cramped quarters and would have aroused the suspicions of our neighbours. The only book in our possession was the German-Jewish joke book, which we quoted from time to time. We may have held on to it as an act of defiance. The tattered volume was as much a telltale sign of our origins as my brother's circumcision. Nevertheless, gallows humour was an important weapon in our fight for survival and allowed us, on rare occasions, to gain some distance from our own situation, which appeared progressively more hopeless. Except for the danger of discovery, our lives in most respects did not seem so very different from those of our neighbours. In the winter of 1944, conditions in Slovakia were chaotic and life was hard for everybody. Most children in the neighbourhood did not attend school or play on the streets. Since food was scarce and tempers were short, socializing was kept to a minimum. But even in the worst of times, neighbours banded together to share news and gossip and to create some sort of self-help community. Hardship may have brought others together, but we were not, nor could we be, included. Our isolation was largely self-inflicted, but it was essential. We were both visible and invisible.

Teta was our eyes and ears to the world. Publicly, her status was that of a refugee from the front lines, the wife of a policeman who was serving in eastern Slovakia, with three children under her care; secretly, she was the guardian of seven people whom she nurtured on meagre food supplies and protected from the ever present danger of discovery, betrayal and death. Although my brother and I had false papers, we did not dare to spend much time outside of our house. Ours was a delicate balancing act. Not appearing at all would have aroused suspicion; exposing ourselves too much would have tempted fate. Vlasta behaved as we did – she did not attend school, she did not form friendships with the neighbourhood children, and she did not spend much time playing on the street.

What I do remember very clearly is the atmosphere of our little house, and how Teta presided over it. I recall her impartiality, her fairness, her ability to distinguish between necessary and unnecessary risks, her talent for dissembling when confronted with hostility, her gift for deflecting suspicion, and her absolute commitment to our survival. Had she not possessed these traits, we would not have escaped discovery. Hence my memories are clustered around what may seem to be the more exceptional, one could even say dramatic, events of our lives together; they provided the texture and reality of our daily existence. Danger was ever present and overshadowed the ordinary features of our lives.

A most basic problem arose on the first day of our life on the Črmáň. The house we rented, like most others in the neighbourhood, had no toilet, only an outhouse in one corner of the garden. This did not present a difficulty to the four official inhabitants of the house, but what of the ones in hiding? Every possible solution carried a risk. To use chamber pots and empty them in the evening may have created a strange odour in our little house, which would not have escaped our neighbours and infrequent visitors; to wait until dark was difficult at all times and occasionally impossible; to hang our laundry in the garden in a way that would obstruct the view of our neighbours and serve as a curtain to the outhouse was, during most of the summer months, possible, but certainly not foolproof. What if the wind blew from an unexpected direction, exposing the movement of people behind the drying sheets? And then, what was one to do on cold and rainy days? Since all the options carried risks, we chose to use all three – depending on the weather and the length of daylight hours. From the distance of over 56 years it may appear somewhat humorous that, day after day, we convened 'high council' to decide how to dispose of human waste. Maybe our focus on such natural and essential functions helped us cope with fear and boredom. We knew that these decisions could be fateful and that any misjudgement would have serious consequences. We lived in a state of 'high alert.'

Despite our cramped quarters and primitive facilities, our hiding place was one of comparative luxury. There were individuals, and even whole families, some with infants, who spent months living in forests, caves, pigsties, cowsheds and abandoned buildings. They could not, as homeless people do today, camp out on public properties or seek shelter in churches. When conditions became physically or psychologically intolerable they had three terrible options – to look for another place, with a high likelihood of failure; to give themselves up; or to commit suicide.

Food was an ever-present problem. Officially, we were entitled to four ration cards – three for children and one for an adult. Yet there were eight people to be fed – five children and three adults. While additional supplies were occasionally available on the black market, shopping 'under the table' was both dangerous and costly. If Teta were caught, or followed home, our cover might be blown. Or we could be betrayed by a peasant who was selling us his provisions and did not like the price we offered, or by another potential buyer whom we had outbid. We constantly balanced the need for more food, the need to husband our resources and the need to avoid being caught in illegal barters. We knew that if the war were to last for another year we would not have enough money to buy even the food to which our ration cards entitled us. While we were not starving, food was scarce and we often went hungry. I remember clearly the night Vlasta and I were sleeping on a small bed under the kitchen window. The day before, Teta had secured – from the black market I am sure – a piece of sausage which she had hung from a hook to let it cure. I can still recapture the smell (very different from Proust's memories of his 'madeleines'!) and our overpowering desire to have just the smallest of tastes, perhaps a piece so tiny that it would not be missed. Maybe, we speculated, we could just touch the sausage and then lick our fingers. Or we could stand on a stool and inhale the intoxicating smells of garlic and spiced lard. I am proud to say we resisted all temptation – not out of fear of punishment (I do not remember any of us ever being punished or reprimanded during the months in hiding), but because we knew the value of even the slightest morsel. And if we were to get any closer to our object of desire than we already were, our hunger might break our resolve not to pilfer, not even a little bit. Weeks later, thin slices of the sausage appeared in our potato dish – we called it *'grulovnick'* – the treat Teta cooked on the days we did our heavy laundry. It probably did not taste quite as good as it would have on the night of our temptation, but Vlasta and I felt we had achieved a moral victory.

In foraging for food, Teta tried to imitate our neighbours. She bought our quota of rationed food, loudly complained about its quality and quantity, and from time to time ventured out to the black market to supplement our meagre provisions. Everything we did had potentially serious consequences, and sometimes it was hard to balance the reality of hunger against the more distant possibility of being caught buying food illegally. There was always the temptation to strike an imaginary bargain: we will go to the black market only one more time, and if we were not caught, we would never go again. We ate what we could get, including horse meat, except for my mother, who could not bring herself to touch non-kosher meat. Everything was divided carefully and fairly. Vlasta never received more than the rest of us. Compared to inmates of concentration camps, workers in forced labour camps, or people hiding in the forest, we lived well; compared to our neighbours, our diet was meagre and insufficient.

During the last few weeks in hiding I suffered from severe boils and sores which, I learned later, were at least partly the result of malnutrition and vitamin deficiency. Despite the prudent husbanding of resources and carefully planned trips to the black market, our financial condition became catastrophic at the same time that our health was breaking down. Left without sufficient funds to supplement our food rations, we were forced to make a decision that involved a big risk for all of us (described in the next chapter). In hindsight, this action brought us large and unexpected benefits, which contributed significantly to our ability to survive the war. But our choice was guided not by wisdom or foresight, but by hunger and despair.

In an effort to save as much money as possible, my brother and I occasionally ventured into the local forests to steal wood, or onto the tracks of the railway station to pick up pieces of coal that had fallen off the railroad cars. While many neighbourhood children engaged in low level pilfering, which by the end of the war had become an accepted way of life, for us there were serious consequences if we were caught and hauled to the police station for questioning. We did not have a 'look-out' to warn us of approaching danger, nor would we have been able to talk ourselves out of it. Even if our false papers could withstand superficial scrutiny, my brother's physiology would instantly give us away. Since it was not customary to circumcise Christian youngsters in Slovakia, pulling down his pants would have provided quick and incontrovertible evidence against him. But as always, Teta encouraged a balancing act – some prudence and some risk taking, hopefully in the right proportions. I believe that she was the only one who knew what my brother and I were up to when we disappeared in the late afternoon – and hence the only one who worried and fretted if we were late getting home. I remember the chilling, damp cold of the winter evenings when we were returning from our forays – but also the sense of triumph when we managed to gather a load that was so heavy we could barely carry it. We had so few ways to contribute to our collective survival that even the smallest success became valued and treasured, both for itself and for the difference it made in our lives.

During the bleakest weeks of the winter of 1944, my brother fell seriously ill and eventually developed pneumonia. Day after day he stayed in bed, his fever climbing to life threatening levels, his eyes glazed, his body visibly wasting. We knew that he was very, very, sick, and we could only hope that he would

not die. There was little we could do to help him. Even if we succeeded in locating a doctor and then found the money to pay for
the house visit, how could we risk exposing his circumcised
body to a physician whose party loyalty, or hatred of Jews,
might trump the Hippocratic Oath of his profession? What now
may be a textbook case in medical ethics was for us a grim reality. On this occasion, we did not use a moral calculus to weigh
the value of possibly saving one life against the risk of exposing
eight people to mortal harm. We did what at the time seemed
the only thing we could do – we watched over him, we provided whatever comfort we could through the use of cold com-
presses and, above all, we continued to hope. My mother, as
always, was in charge of prayers. We tried the local pharmacist,
but he had no medication that would suppress the fever or act
as a palliative for the symptoms. I remember a terrible thought I
had one night. What would we do if my brother died? How
would we dispose of his body? How would we account for his
absence? How would we hide our grief? Watching helplessly as
he fought for his life and thinking the unthinkable may have
helped me to cope with the frightening reality that I may lose
him. But Teta did not give up easily. She took one of her less and
less frequent trips to the black market and came back with milk
and eggs. Abandoning the general rule of sharing everything
equally, she reserved these delicacies for my brother who, alas,
had to be cajoled into taking them. I do not believe that any of
us could have accepted even a small portion of the food, had it
been offered to us. By giving him eggs and milk we felt that we
were doing something that might make him better, that we were
no longer helpless bystanders and that he was not doomed to
die. A few days later, my brother started a slow but steady recovery. To this day I believe that he was saved by the magic potion
of milk, eggs, courage and love.

My parents, sister and cousin spent most of the daylight
hours in the attic. The floors and walls were paper thin, without
any insulation, and their slightest movement, or their quietest
whispers, reverberated throughout the house. Since it was winter and the windows were closed, there were no outside noises
to block out the sounds emanating from the attic. On the rare
occasions when we had visitors (almost always unannounced)
the inhabitants of the attic 'froze' in their positions and did not

utter a word. We did our best to distract the visitors with loud talk, laughter, the clatter of dishes and a blaring radio to drown out any sounds that might come from above. At times, when, despite their best efforts, their movements could be heard downstairs, at least by us, who knew of their existence, the tension we felt was close to unbearable. It would have been just as easy to betray ourselves by the fear in our eyes as through the unexplained movements above our heads. One serious problem was my mother's terror of mice, which expressed itself in an involuntary cry which she could try to muffle but could not suppress. There was no way we could win the war against the mice. They bred more quickly than we could catch them, and they lived in the attic. The thought of being betrayed by a mouse was both grotesque and real. My father was alert to the danger, and kept his hand ready to put over my mother's mouth before a cry could escape. I have 'inherited' a fear of mice, but my instinctive response to this day is to freeze on the spot and not move until the little creature is caught, or, after taking one look at me, runs away. I may have quietly practised this response while listening to my mother's muffled cries from the attic.

Our difficulties were endless and the dangers of discovery ever present. Despite our best efforts to blend into the neighbourhood, rumours that Jews were hiding in the house began to circulate soon after we moved in. At first we tried to ignore them, hoping that it was a distrust of strangers, rather than any specific suspicions about us, that fuelled the talk. But the whispering persisted, and it became only a matter of time before the neighbours would launch a full-scale investigation, undoubtedly with assistance from the local police and the Hlinka Guard. It was clear to us that the hatred of Jews, combined with a more general xenophobia and a love of gossip, created an explosive situation, which required that we go on the offensive. Easier said than done. How could we defend ourselves against accusations that were correct and could so easily be verified?

Before we could decide on our next move, our landlady, who was employed as a chambermaid in a local hotel, appeared suddenly on our doorstep and made it clear that she came to conduct what turned out to be a very public inspection of her house. Well known in the neighbourhood, her announcement that she had taken a day off work to investigate whether there was any truth to the rumours that Jews were living in her house was warmly applauded by the people on our street. Armed with a loud voice and an ample bosom, her entrance was fierce and dramatic. To make sure that there were many witnesses to this spectacle, she opened all the doors and windows so that the neighbours could see and hear what was going on inside. She came prepared to slay the dragons (exterminate vermin may be a more appropriate metaphor) who took over her house. Faced with the inevitable, Teta too assumed a highly dramatic posture. In a mocking voice and with large operatic gestures sweeping over the tiny spaces of the house, she encouraged the landlady to look around. The land-lady was enthusiastic in her search. She looked under the beds, opened all the closet doors, pulled out every drawer in sight (she may even have opened the oven door), and rummaged through the pantry, all the while proclaiming loudly that she would not tolerate the presence of Jews in her house, and that if she found any she would instantly turn them over to the police. Her search was accompanied by loud and profuse cursing of the whole tribe of Israel. Teta joined her in her diatribe and egged her on. We were mesmerized by the performance of the two furies, but we were absolutely convinced that the play would soon be over and that all would be lost. Within minutes, all eight of us would be standing in front of the house, exposed and defenceless. To our great astonishment, the landlady, after a thorough examination of the shelves and cupboards in the pantry, neglected to climb up the steps that led to the attic. Could she have forgotten that part of the house? Was she so preoccupied with the drama of the inspection that she overlooked the obvious? We did not discover the reason for our miraculous reprieve until the last few days of the war (discussed in the next chapter). Unbeknownst to them-selves, both Teta and the landlady were engaged in a deadly game of deceit. Both knew something and had something to hide, but neither knew everything. The visit had long lasting beneficial effects. The neighbours were satisfied that the rumours they heard, and helped to spread, were unfounded. Teta walked around with her head held high and with a look of reproach for those who were vile enough to accuse her of harbouring Jews. There was a temporary peace in the neighbourhood.

During the months in hiding, we took one enormous and unnecessary risk and I am not sure why my father and Teta

allowed it. Ever since I can remember, my parents were avid
newspaper readers and radio listeners. I can still see the large
volumes of bound old newspapers on our bookshelves in
Prešov, collected by my father year after year. When Jews were
no longer allowed to possess radios, somehow we held on to
ours. Now, in virtual captivity, our only connection with the outside world was through the radio. Teta was, of course, allowed
to have a radio, so that did not present a problem. But every day
at the appointed time, with windows and doors locked, we huddled around the wireless and listened to the forbidden BBC
voice. Still today, whenever I listen to hourly news reports, I half
expect to hear the opening bars of Beethoven's Fifth Symphony
that preceded the wartime broadcasts. To us, they signalled not
the promise of a rich musical experience, but the imminent presence of a voice that would connect us to another world; a world
in which humanity and decency were the norm, a world which
reminded us of our past and, for a brief moment, liberated us
from the oppression of the present. The radio was our window
to the future – if there was to be a future for us. We heard what
we longed to hear – that the defeat of Germany was certain, that
its surrender would be unconditional, and that the punishment
of collaborators would be swift and severe. What we did not
hear was when the hour of our liberation would come; a point
in time toward which we could start our countdown. The fact
that Germany had lost the war did not mean that we were
saved. On the contrary, new dangers appeared every day,
including last minute aerial bombings or final sweeps to ferret
out all the enemies of the Reich and of the independent Slovak
State. Although we did not know it then, such senseless, desperate, last minute murders happened routinely on the 'death
marches' out of concentration camps on the eve of their liberation by allied soldiers. Yet we were immeasurably cheered by
news of the imminent and inevitable defeat of Germany and by
the reassurance that the madness that had engulfed so much of
our world for so many years would soon come to an end. We
lived on two planes. On one plane, every day, like every flip of
a coin, presented the same chances of being caught and executed. If anything, the chances would increase if, because of our
hope, we were to let up on our vigilance, or because of their fury,
our enemies were to make a last ditch effort to find and kill all

Knowledge / connection w/ o/s world .

remaining Jews. On another plane, we could start to hope that we were surviving not just for another hour, another day, or another week, but for a new and safe life. After six years of persecutions we could no longer imagine what our ordinary life would be, and we had terrifying premonitions of the losses we would discover after the war. We did not anticipate a return to the world as we had known it, but, despite our fears, we retained some hope about the world to come.

We left our little house on the Črmáň about a week before liberation, some time during the last week of March. Without Teta's heroic efforts we would have been deported in October 1944. Without the help of our next door neighbours on the Črmáň, to whom we turned for help at the very end of the war, we would probably have been exposed and executed in late March 1945. What follows is the story of those neighbours: Michael Laco and his wife, Margareta Lacová, a sister-in-law, Pani Eperješová (our landlady), a brother-in-law, Rudolf Valent, and the latter's friend, William Koenig, both of whom worked with the underground.

hope for the world to come

1. In addition to the knowledge of the o/s world through radio.

2. The warm comfort of family — all immediates present

3. Eva + brother's: false birth records allowed some escape from house.

6 Descent into the Underground

The last few months in hiding had the character, if not then, certainly in retrospect, of a race against time with a very uncertain outcome. Although we knew that the defeat of Germany was inevitable, and we could see the finish line, our lives became daily more precarious and our survival less certain. The immediate threat to us came from two fronts. With rapidly dwindling funds, we were worried about our ability to purchase even our meagre rations, and we were reluctant to spend money on much needed food supplies still available on the black market. Secondly, even if we could physically hold out, we did not know how to prepare for the long awaited final battle for Nitra. If, before the arrival of the Russian troops, the town were to be bombed or subjected to artillery fire, as happened in many other cities in eastern Slovakia, we might be forced out of our house and thus fall prey to hostile neighbours and whatever local militia was still around. Our persecutors also could see the finish line, but it made them only more ferocious and intent on revenge. It is no sweeter to die at the moment of liberation than it is at any other time. Thus, on one side we saw the promise of life, on the other side the real threat of extreme hunger and violent death. Even this late in the game, no wise person would have given us unequivocal advice or taken a bet on the outcome.

A great deal has been written about the passivity of the victims – their lack of will, or ability, or strength of character, or all of those taken together, to defend themselves and fight for their survival. Then there are the counter-arguments of those who point to the heroic resistance of individuals and groups who did battle, at times to save themselves, at times to shield others, and at times to lock in mortal combat with the enemy, letting death embrace both. Yet others offer plausible explanations for the seeming paralysis of the victims by pointing to the diabolical and successful schemes of the Nazi regimes to strip those they

persecuted of all vestiges of humanity. Deprived of their citizenship, forbidden to practice their professions, subjected to
arbitrary edicts, separated from their family and left without
even the most basic material possessions, they lost their sense of
'place,' and their membership in the human community. There
is some truth in all of these accounts, but they are incomplete,
largely written by outsiders who themselves are strangers to the
experiences on which they are passing judgement. In any case,
these broad generalizations do not exhaust the range of
responses of the victims, who continued to invent, and reinvent,
strategies to deal with their changing circumstances. For many
who went into hiding, every day was a fight for survival, moti-
vated not only by the will to live, but also by a will to defy the
enemy and to deprive him of his bounty. Viewed from a
historical perspective, it may be hard to understand how much
courage it took to keep on inventing adequate defences for living another day or another week.

the hiding life

In the late winter of 1944 and early spring of 1945, when the
end of our suffering and the defeat of the enemy seemed so
close, we were energized to action, determined to beat the odds
that we would not survive. While these actions involved additional risks, they also held out the promise that we would reach
the finish line. Our determination grew in proportion to the
threats we were facing.

Our next door neighbours on Čulenova ulica were a childless
couple, Pán Laco and his wife, Pani Lacová. Their house was
much more spacious than ours. The front of the house was occupied by a small grocery store, which they owned. For reasons I
no longer know (if ever I did), they were the only neighbours
with whom we felt comfortable. During the winter months, my
brother and I would visit them from time to time. Although they
were not used to the company of children, they made us feel
welcome and at ease, offering us sweets and soft drinks. They
asked no questions about why we came to Nitra and showed no
curiosity about our family situation or the details of our daily
lives. Occasionally they were joined by two young male visitors,
whom they introduced as Rudolf Valent, a brother-in-law, and
his friend, William Koenig. These two men never stayed long,
nor did they engage in chitchat. The reason for their presence
was not clear to us, although we sensed that these were not

The children to whom we carry messages to the words

ordinary familial or social visits. From time to time, when my brother and I set out foraging for wood in god-forsaken places, Rudolf and William would ask us to drop off a written message at some appointed place (never to deliver it to a person). We did what we were asked to do, and did not inquire about the content of the messages or about the people for whom they were destined. Although totally ignorant of the cause we might have been serving, we sensed that these messages were important and that they created an additional danger for us in case we were caught stealing. We were also convinced that we were participating in something that was larger than our own lives, and that what we were asked to do was in some way related to our hopes for liberation. We felt both frightened and strong.

When our food situation became extreme, the adults in our house decided, who knows on the basis of what odds, that Teta would tell the Lacos, with as little detail as possible, that eight people were living in the house next to them, and that we were in need of food. As owners of a small grocery store, they had well-established connections with peasants in the countryside who brought them eggs, milk, cheese and other fresh produce. They would thus be in a position to help us, provided they were willing to do so. They could, of course, refuse to become involved, and worse than that, they could betray us. At least, to some extent, their kindness to my brother and me, and even the 'mysterious messages' we were asked to deliver, helped us make the decision. We still had in our possession a large gold bracelet, dating back to times we could hardly remember, and we were ready to offer it in exchange for food. I do not know what the Lacos' response to Teta was, or whether they registered a great deal of surprise when they were told that a large family lived next door to them. I know that they did not accept the bracelet, since it remains the only piece of family jewellery that survived the war. I also know that without our revelation and their willingness to help, we might not have survived. While food continued to be scarce, we now could supplement the meagre rations for four to which we were entitled with supplies from the larders of the Lacos' grocery store. I do not believe that the gift of food was preceded by a meeting of our two families, or that they even knew a great deal about us. As a general rule, one did not exchange more information than was absolutely necessary. The less one knew, the less one would have to reveal under questioning. Ignorance was a safety valve against forced betrayal.

Pán Laco and Pani Lacová were willing to share with us not only food, but also shelter. They told us that if, for whatever reason, we had to leave our house, and if we could escape unnoticed, we could move into their air raid shelter. That was an incredibly generous offer, since we expected that the final days of the battle for Nitra would be accompanied by heavy bombardments, forcing people either into a basement (which we did not have) or a public shelter (which we could not use).

Under their living room floor, Pán Laco and Pani Lacová were building an underground bunker that could house more than a dozen people. They did not tell us, and we did not ask, why they needed such a large space, since there were only the two of them and it was to be a very temporary shelter against aerial attacks, rather than a fully fledged hiding place. Within a few days, my brother and I were invited to help build the 'safe house.' Every night, when the neighbours around us slept, we dug deep under the floor of the living room and carried bucketfuls of earth a fair distance from the house, so as not to have suspicious mounds of freshly dug up earth next to the Lacos' dwelling. In our nocturnal work, we were often joined by Pán Valent and Pán Koenig, who contributed construction tools, muscle power, expertise, and a sense of humour. They would disappear as mysteriously as they appeared. Every day at dawn, the large section of the living room floor that we had cut out was put back and camouflaged by a rug and a heavy piece of furniture. The work was backbreaking, but we made progress. We shared a sense of adventure (my brother and I were of the age when playing hide and seek, or cops and robbers, still had fascination) and we were proud to be treated as equals in an important undertaking. Although we maintained our false identities – I was Magda and my brother was Toni – we were not required to play-act or to keep exchanges brief and noncommittal. Whoever we might be, we were shown kindness and acceptance, with no questions asked. While the Lacos had not met our parents or sister or cousin, they knew that eight people were living next door to them, that four of them did not have ration cards, and that all of them might soon come to the underground shelter. Minimal knowledge and maximal help were the rule of thumb.

One of my most vivid memories of that period is of an evening when a few German soldiers in an already inebriated state came into the store, and asked for drinks. With great merriment they put on the radio and demanded that the women who were present dance with them. I was fourteen, Pani Lacová probably about thirty-five. To refuse was not an option. But as I danced with the soldiers to the tune of some sentimental waltz, instead of feeling frightened and angry, I felt smug and triumphant every time we came close to the covered up hole in the living room floor. What sweet satisfaction came from the feeling that just beneath their dancing feet was our escape route of which they knew nothing. Perhaps I was able to dance, and to smile, because I knew that they were fooled. Had they known who we were, they might have liked to dance on our graves; instead, they danced on our road to freedom. And I knew that Pani Lacová was on my side, and that helped immensely. Two females, one still a child, one a mature woman, playing a trick on enemy soldiers. After the soldiers left, we refrained from discussing our feelings.

Hard as we tried to accomplish our task, it took several weeks to build the shelter. We had to take breaks, both because there were days when the earth was frozen and we could not dig, and because some of the work was so hard that we needed the help of Pán Valent and Pán Koenig, who were only occasionally present. Once the basic structure was finished, we started to 'furnish' the space with mattresses, shelves, a short wave radio, batteries, drinking water, and as many cans of food as we could take off the grocery shelves without leaving gaping holes. We were careful and methodical. Concentrating on the details may have helped us to forget that the bunker was built with the worst possible scenarios in mind. As I write about those days, I think of my paternal grandmother who, every summer, would make containers of jams and preserves, mumbling to herself *'man soll's nicht brochen'* (you should not need it). These delicacies were offered to us only when we were sick. Perhaps not dispensing them freely was her way of warding off sickness and the evil spirits who cause it. The bunker too, with what seemed its plentiful emergency food supply, fell into the *'man soll's nicht brochen'* category. I do not remember ever being tempted to swipe a can of food, though I knew that it would not be missed. Maybe I was just exercising the self-restraint I learned the night when the smell of the sausage hanging from the window wafted into the bed Vlasta and I shared. It is more likely that I was overcome with the responsibility of creating a shelter for our survival, and that I would do nothing that would, in the least, diminish its effectiveness.

It is hard to describe the sense of freedom and satisfaction we derived from building the bunker and stocking it with items we needed for survival. Every time we carried out a bucket of earth, fastened the shelves to the walls, created ducts for ventilation or added candles or little oil lamps, we felt like soldiers preparing for the last battle. We had no guns or tanks to fight our enemies, but perhaps we had the wit, the will and the stamina to outsmart and to outlast them. While Teta and Vlasta kept their responsibilities for our everyday lives, my brother and I helped to provide for the future. By enlarging the circle of our saviours we felt less vulnerable and less alone.

The time to move to the bunker came in the last week of March, when the Russian Army was poised on the outskirts of Nitra and the sound of artillery fire reverberated through our little house. How we managed to get my parents, sister and cousin from our house to the house next door, or which of our meagre possessions we took with us, I do not remember. Nor do I remember how we succeeded in disappearing from our house without arousing the suspicion of our other neighbours. It is hard to understand how so much detailed planning and careful scheming leaves no memory traces. I can imagine several scenarios. For the first few days we could have stayed in our house during the day and only slept in the bunker. Or perhaps my parents and sister and cousin moved there, and the four 'legitimate' inhabitants of our house moved in later, when the whole city was in chaos and people found refuge wherever they could. It is also possible that we all waited together until just before the town was to be captured, and then left for the bunker.

While I do not remember our arrival, I remember vividly both our stay in the underground hiding place and our staged departures several days later. My brother, Vlasta, Teta and I emerged shortly after the town was liberated by the Russian Army. My parents, sister and cousin stayed a couple more days – in case the town changed hands again, as happened not infrequently, and they would have been exposed. The closer we came to liberation, the more fearful we became of an accident that would betray us. The more focused the danger, the more the odds seemed against us. Or perhaps we became more cautious because we now had hope of success and a sense that we could help write the ending of the script. While some facts have been buried in the deep recesses of my memory, what is very vivid to me is the atmosphere of careful deliberation and calculation before we made a move.

buried facts

There was something reassuring about the bunker. Dark, damp, under the ground, and built as a hiding place, it seemed infinitely safer than our house, with its doors, windows, neighbours, and a forced appearance of normalcy, had ever been. Now we did not have to pretend that we were just an ordinary family living as best we could in war-torn Nitra. We lived like animals, under the earth; the hunted trying to escape the hunter. It was more than just feeling safer; we also felt that we had stopped living a lie.

feeling safer under-ground

Shortly after we arrived in the bunker we were joined by Pán Koenig and Pán Valent. Their presence provided comfort and reassurance. Pán Laco and Pani Lacová stayed in their house and continued their normal routines, only venturing down from time to time to bring us some fresh food and water so that we would conserve our supplies, or to share with us the latest rumours. We lived with a sense of quiet before the storm. What we did not know was whether fair winds or ill winds would blow our way. As it so often turns out in life, both fair and ill winds came our way.

Late one evening, a couple of days after our move to the bunker, the landlady of our Črmáň house – the one who had carried out such a thorough public inspection in order to make sure that no Jews were occupying the premises – arrived at her brother-in-law's house with three people in tow. She showed little surprise at seeing all eight of us there. Once the introductions were made (at this stage of the game with real names, except for my brother and me, who remained Tony Kašprišin and Magda Kašprišinová), we discovered that the family of three she had brought with her – and for whom we were, unbeknownst to us, also building the bunker – was that of a local Jewish dentist, his wife and teen-age son. Since we had not lived in Nitra until shortly before we went into hiding, we did not know them and they did not know us. This is their story. Since the head of household was a dentist and his functions were deemed essential, he was allowed to stay in Nitra until the fall of 1944. On the morning of the final roundup of Jews, at about the same time that my father and sister set out for the hiding place on the Črmáň, the dentist and his family moved into the small, cramped hotel room which Pani Eperješová was given as part of her chambermaid's compensation. The plans had been made some time earlier, but as in our case, they were executed in a hurry. Pani Eperješová's well-publicized visit to our house, and her noisy and seemingly thorough inspection of it to ferret out any Jews who might be hiding in it, served a double purpose. In the first place, it earned her credentials as a true-blooded hater of Jews; a useful attribution for a woman sheltering a Jewish family. In the second place, it served to quiet the rumour that she had been duped and that in addition to the four inhabitants to whom she had rented her house, there were Jews hiding in it. We knew how difficult it was to mask the presence of four additional people in a small house; it is almost inconceivable that four people could have stayed in a single room in a public building for all these months without giving themselves away. Even if she was the only chambermaid living in the attic of the hotel with no immediate next door neighbours, it is difficult to fathom how the dentist and his family managed to escape detection. Did Pani Eperješová pilfer food from the hotel kitchen to feed them? Did she receive help from the Lacos or from the Slovak Underground? One can invoke luck, or fate. It would be unseemly to give credit to divine providence without confronting the question – why were so many destroyed, and so few saved? Surely the answer could not be based on a comprehensible notion of divine justice or on individual merit. Ivan's challenge to his brother, Alyosha (*The Brothers Karamazov*), when he asks him to explain how, in a just world, one can account for the suffering of one innocent child, would have to be multiplied many times over.

In the evening, when 16 people were assembled in the bunker (the eight of us, our hosts, Pán Valent and Pán Koenig

74

and Pani Eperješová with her three 'guests'), it seemed to us that all the good people of the town, and all the Jews who had thus far survived in Nitra, were in the same place. While objectively this was not true, that thought had a powerful subjective reality. We were a small, very special community – 16 ordinary people – many of whom did not know each other before the war and would go their separate ways after the war.

It is easy to recapture the sense of camaraderie and loyalty that bound us to each other during the final days of the war. It is much harder to understand how it came about that we scattered after our liberation. There are, of course, explanations. People moved. Circumstances after the war were chaotic and remained unsettled for a very long time. All of us needed to forget the past in order to create a future. My mother, my brother and sister and I left for America and my father went to Israel. I believe Pán Koenig and Pán Valent became important officials in the Czechoslovak Government after the communist take-over in 1948, and they may have helped us once more when we needed to get out of the country. I do not know whether they were ultimately caught in the purges inside the communist party after 1948 or in the crossfires of the Slansky trials in 1952, when many former party members were accused of bourgeois treachery. In hindsight, there are many explanations that satisfy reason, but they do not address the concerns of the heart or the spirit. I know that during the days and nights the 16 of us, ten adults and six children, spent in the bunker, not one of us could have conceived of a time when we would no longer be connected or willing to help one another.

I do not know how many days and nights we spent in the bunker, but I know that we were never in danger of running out of food or other essential supplies. Huddled in our small quarters, we listened to the interrupted and unreliable Slovak news reports and to the more reliable sounds of bombardment and artillery as they came closer and closer to us. We rejoiced when the hits were so close that our canned food rolled off the shelves and the floor above us rocked. We were very quiet, as if reluctant to call attention to ourselves, but for us, each hit signified not so much mortal danger as imminent liberation. After each explosion we listened to the rumbling noise of shattered buildings and felled trees. Occasionally, we heard sirens wailing in the distance, but they were few and far between. The infrastructure of the city of Nitra had collapsed.

With the arrival of the Russian Army in Nitra, we were, after six years of harassment and persecutions, free. Yet we did not know what we should do or where we should go. We did not know who would be in charge, and how we would identify ourselves, since months before we had left all our official documents behind. After waiting so long for our liberation, when it came, we did not know how to act. So, once again, we exercised extreme caution.

During the first few days after the battle for Nitra, when Teta, Vlasta, my brother and I emerged from the bunker, we retained our fictitious identities. Only days later, when Nitra was securely in the hands of the Russian Army, did the two Jewish families leave the bunker. It was one of the great ironies of fate that when I finally told our neighbours that my real name was not Magda Kašprišinová but Eva Reinitzová, they refused to believe me. They were suspicious – perhaps we had something to hide and were now assuming 'false' identities. The emergence of our parents and sister only confirmed for them that what they had suspected for a long time was true, and what, after the public inspection of our house they had accepted as truth, was false. I remember their surprise. I do not remember that they were pleased that we had managed to survive. Maybe they were indignant that they had been duped; or fearful that we would turn against them and report their threats and suspicions; or perhaps they were disappointed that we were alive; or they may have been simply so busy with their own daily lives and hardships that they had no feelings to spare. I remember a sense of relief, but not of triumph. We were out of danger, but also rootless and homeless.

It would be nice to remember the days of liberation as festivals of rebirth, with songs and dance and sounds of trumpets. But that was not the case. More modestly, we would have been delighted to find ourselves transported magically to the pre-war days in Prešov, to resume our daily routines and activities – to awake from a nightmare and find the world as we left it six years before. Instead, we found ourselves disoriented, devastated by our gradual discovery of the enormity of the destruction of our community and our extended family (much worse than we had expected), fearful of the present and uncertain about the future. For months, we had dreamt of the day when we would come out of hiding and resume our lives. We knew that we could not turn back the clock and recapture our pre-war existence, but we hoped to find enough familiar markers and signposts to give us a new start. Reality was harsher and more complex than we had anticipated. We were grateful to be alive, but neither jubilant nor quietly contented. The weeks after the war brought their own anxieties, uncertainties and dangers – some of them life threatening. During the war, we were classified as a racial minority singled out for extinction. After the war, we became, ironically, part of the conquered population that had to be punished for its co-operation with the German Reich. Our neighbours were not pleased that we survived – and our liberators treated us as citizens of a conquered country. It took us months to find our bearings again and to establish some sort of normal life – and even that turned out to be only temporary.

Several weeks after our liberation, we said good bye to Pán Laco and Pani Lacová and moved from our house on the Črmáň back to the town of Nitra. Our lodgings were temporary; only a way station to what we hoped to be a more settled and permanent existence. Shortly after we moved in, my father travelled to Košice in the hope of finding a sufficiently large Jewish community which we could join, and where perhaps he could find a position similar to the one he held in Prešov before the war. This was our first tentative step toward re-establishing a normal existence. My mother and Teta were left in charge of Greta, Vlasta and the three of us.

If there was any place in Slovakia where there was hope of rebuilding a Jewish community, Košice seemed a promising destination. A large provincial town, dominated by a cathedral and an opera house, about thirty miles south of Prešov, it had been ceded to Hungary in the 1939 exchange of territories, and then returned to the Czechoslovak Republic in 1945. Before the war, Košice had roughly 70,000 thousand inhabitants, of whom about 12,500, or 18 per cent, were Jews. Because the deportations of Jews from Košice, as from the rest of Hungary, did not start until the summer of 1944, a relatively large number survived the war. While, over the years, emigration and natural attrition have taken their toll, even in 1993, when we visited Košice, it still had, with about three hundred Jewish families, the second largest concentration of Jews in Slovakia, right after Bratislava.

My father's hopes were not disappointed. Within a few days of his arrival in Košice, he was invited to take a leadership role in rebuilding the Jewish community. He started his task with a certain amount of optimism, only to be disappointed three and a half years later, when he had to leave Slovakia and move to Israel. But at the time, he believed that in Košice we could rebuild our personal and communal lives.

7 Months of Uncertainty

Even under ideal circumstances, it would have been difficult to recreate a semblance of the life we had left behind six years ago. In fairy tales, princes or princesses emerge from a long sleep more beautiful than ever, and take their rightful place in a world that is warm and welcoming. In real life, things are different and much more difficult. The years of hiding had scarred us and left us uncertain about our identities and our place in the shattered world of post-war Slovakia. Without clearly recognizing it at the time, each one of us, adults and children, had been deeply marked by our experiences. We could try to forget them or perhaps transcend them, but we could not erase them. Our personal transformations, or more precisely deformations, were more than matched by the contours of the world we re-entered. Both the private familial realm and the communal realm had undergone vast changes. Almost all our relatives on my father's side, and most of our friends, young and old, were dead; our community was decimated; we had lost our possessions and our sense of belonging. My mother's immediate family was more fortunate. Her five siblings, two of them with husbands and children, scattered shortly before the war: two went to America; one went to England, where he was interned on the Isle of Man as an enemy alien; one spent the war in hiding in the mountains of Italy; and one served in the Palestinian brigade of the British Army. Her mother was sheltered by successive Dutch families and moved to America after the war. Her extended family, grandparents, aunts, uncles, cousins, was decimated. A recently discovered letter she wrote to her siblings in America in the fall of 1945 brought back in full force, with specific names and faces, the enormity of the losses in her family. This, roughly translated from German, is how she describes the fate of her maternal grandfather. I believe that the emotionless prose reveals, more powerfully than any lamentation, the depth of the pain.

Unfortunately Grandfather did not escape deportation. Eyewitnesses report that he entered the box cart that carried him to Oswieczim [Auschwitz] erect and with dignity. There he received a blow on his head from SS Rohling of which he died three days later...Unfortunately he had to live to be ninety-three years old to meet such an end. Supposedly, the Christian inhabitants of Nové Zamky presented a petition to save him from deportation (he was the rabbi of the town), but the Gestapo paid no attention. Šari (his daughter) accompanied him on this difficult journey.

When people survive a natural disaster – an earthquake, a plague, a flood, or even a war – they tend to come together in a common endeavour to rebuild from the ruins. We had the ruins, but we lacked the human and material resources to build on them, or even to start anew. Emerging from hiding, we were welcomed neither by the local population, who regarded us as disturbing ghosts from a past they wanted to forget (though they wanted to keep the possessions that were left behind), nor by the conquering army, for whom we were indistinguishable from the enemy. In a totally irrational, but perhaps psychologically understandable way, the civilian population blamed us for the physical hardship now imposed on it – as if the Russian Army had come for the express purpose of liberating us. But neither were we the 'chosen people' for the conquering army. The Russian soldiers distinguished between the people they had fought bitterly and on whom they now felt entitled to take revenge, and those few others, many of them communists, who had led the short lived partisan uprising in the fall of 1944, whom they trusted and to whom they were prepared to assign official positions. There was no place or privilege, however, for the people who emerged from hiding or who had wandered back, disoriented and despairing, from forced labour centres or from concentration camps. For the Russians we were Slovaks and for the Slovaks we remained Jews. Teta and Vlasta became indistinguishable from the Jews because they had proclaimed their solidarity with us. The best we could hope for was indifference from both the victors and the vanquished and an absence of harm. There were few helping hands or welcoming words. But there were some, and they mattered a great deal.

As our tale of hardship extends into the first few months of liberation, so does the role of people who, during that period, showed us extraordinary kindness. While their acts were significantly different from those of the people to whom we owe our survival, they too belong to the story of 'good beyond evil'. We probably would have survived without them, but by reaching out to us they gave us both the courage and the will to go on. They made us feel that our survival had meaning, that our lives had value, and that we had not struggled through the war only to be confronted by a hostile or indifferent world. What follows in the next two chapters is my memory of five such individuals – a Russian officer, a Russian doctor, a man about whom I know absolutely nothing, a half mad woman who came to stay with us shortly after our liberation and a Carmelite nun.

****

A few days after we left the bunker, on the last day of the Passover holiday, we had an unexpected visit from a Russian officer, dressed in a uniform covered with medals and decorations. How or why he came to us I do not know, although it seems unlikely that he was just strolling around in our working class neighbourhood and happened to knock on our door. The visit may have been a random military check. It is also possible that he came to the house because he had heard that Jews were living in it. Whatever the reason, he did not offer explanations for his visit, nor did we ask. Initially, our conversation was halting, in a mixture of Slovak, Russian, Yiddish and body language. After hearing a bit about who we were and how we survived the war, he shared with us his own sad story.

Shortly after he left for the front in the fall of 1941, he learned that his wife and children, together with many other relatives and friends, had been murdered in the Ukraine by the invading German Army with the help of the local population. Thenceforth he had one goal: to take no prisoners and to kill as many of the enemy as possible. He made no secret of the fact that the rules of military engagement did not apply to him, and that he was driven by hate and revenge. For him, the war was not only a clash of two armies, or a confrontation of two political systems,

81

or even a fight between the forces of good and evil; it was, in the most primitive sense, a matter of personal vengeance for the death of his family and the annihilation of his community. It therefore did not come as a surprise when, after sharing with us the story of his loss and grief, he asked my father, in a matter of fact voice, how many Germans or local collaborators he had killed. When he was told that my father had not killed anyone, he shook his head in disbelief. He may have been shocked not so much by the fact that my father had not destroyed even a single enemy, which could have been ascribed to our circumstances, as by the lack of regret or apology in his response. I will always hear the sob in his voice when, after drinking heavily from the flask of vodka he had brought with him he said, in Yiddish, 'And still I cannot forget'. Neither vodka, nor our presence, nor the end of the war, could touch his pain. Maybe his only palliative was a relentless pursuit of revenge. His parting words to us, late in the day, were that he would never forget that he spent the last day of Passover in the spring of 1945 in Slovakia, with an intact Jewish family of five.

Shortly after his arrival in our midst, the officer commanded a group of soldiers to find a piano and bring it to our house. Since looting was the order of the day, it was not difficult to find a serviceable piano (although perhaps not in our immediate neighbourhood) or even to transport it to our house. The seemingly insurmountable obstacle was the narrow door of our very modest house. Workers' cottages were not built to accommodate pianos. When, after much pushing and shoving, the feat was accomplished, he asked us to open all the doors and windows. We understood the reason for his request when he sat down at the piano and began to play, and sing, old Yiddish melodies – lullabies, children's songs, dance songs, love songs and songs of longing for lost Jerusalem. It is hard to describe the poignancy of the moment. For months we had lived, both literally and figuratively, with closed doors and windows, hiding our Jewishness. Now the neighbours were gathered outside, drawn no doubt by curiosity and some perhaps by envy, listening to the words and melodies of a world that had been destroyed, and yet had, at least momentarily, survived in their midst. As darkness fell and our neighbours dispersed, the officer continued to sing, to play and to drink. Late that night, when he left our house, he was still sad and his memories unredeemed. He had never had the chance to mourn for those he loved – only to avenge them. He was not drunk.

Over the years, I have thought of him often – an officer without a name, with a sad face, a beautiful voice, and rage in his heart. Did he remember us, as he said he would, as the intact Jewish family with whom he spent the last day of Passover in 1945? Did he return to the Ukraine? What was his 'homecoming' like? Did he ever feel his Jewishness with the same ferocity and pain as he did on that afternoon? Did he ever know how much his presence meant to us? And if he did, did it comfort him? Would we have anything to say to each other if we were to meet now – he a very old man and I a not much younger woman? Did he ever forget? I doubt it. Did he find a measure of peace? I hope so.

****

If a Russian officer helped to heal our spirit, a Russian doctor probably saved my life. What is memorable about him is, however, not the way he treated my body, but the care and compassion he showed during the week of my convalescence. Only a few months before, when my brother was gravely ill, we had not dared to ask for medical help for fear that we would be betrayed by the very person whose profession was to heal and to do no harm. By the end of the war, we had so completely lost our trust in human decency and benevolence that every act of kindness and concern had a powerfully healing effect on us. Our moral order was still reversed: we expected evil and were surprised by the good.

Toward the end of the war, I must have suffered, unbeknownst to me or anyone else, from a severe vitamin deficiency. (Perhaps we were protected from knowledge of things we had no power to change.) In the early spring of 1945, the ugly sores I had developed on both my legs, from the knees to the calves, got progressively worse and would not heal, regardless of the home remedies we applied to them. Without strong disinfectants it was almost impossible to keep the affected areas clean. Coarse soap and water were not enough, especially once we started building the bunker. Night after night, as we carried our pails of earth, it was inevitable that some of it landed in my wounds. Washing and scrubbing was painful, and it appeared to make matters worse. The sores became increasingly bothersome and ominous looking. They were so ugly I could not bear to look at them. I distanced myself as best I could both from my pain and from my limbs.

A few days after our liberation, my brother and I ventured to town in search of a military medical facility. Perhaps it was our mistrust of the local hospital that kept us from going there; or we may have thought that the military hospital would have a better supply of medicines. We found one not too far from our Črmáň house – filled with both civilians and soldiers waiting patiently for medical attention. When my turn came, I was assigned to a gruff looking army doctor. He took one look at my legs, then at my face, and said matter of factly, 'This will hurt'. He was true to his words. His method may have been primitive, but it was effective. He soaked some clean rags with a disinfectant, and then started scrubbing my legs, lingering both over the open wounds and those that had developed scabs. It hurt so much that despite my determination to be brave, tears were rolling down my cheeks. But I neither cried nor protested, knowing full well that he did not have a choice about the method of treatment and that he did the best he could without the help of anaesthesia. Even after 55 years, I still remember the smell of the disinfectant and the touch of his hands. I must have been surprised that a big person could have such a gentle touch. Despite the crowded conditions of the outpatient clinic, he did not seem to be in a hurry. Satisfied that he had cleaned the wounds, he patted my head and gave me a supply of pills, probably an early version of antibiotics. Before he sent us on our way he warned my brother that I would have difficulty walking and that I would need to be helped to reach our house. He had no vehicle to spare. I am quite certain that the pills he counted out so carefully were worth their weight in gold and had to be distributed fairly and judiciously.

Our trip across the bridge to the Črmáň was difficult. I was in considerable pain and I had to walk on bare feet because the sandals I had worn to town would no longer fit. I hobbled and cried all the way. That relatively short journey has served as a benchmark for physical pain that I experienced later in life, not because it was so intense, but because, for the first time in years, I was allowed to express it without fear of consequences. During the war, illness always meant added vulnerability and danger; now it was just something that had to be endured, and that would pass.

That evening, to our great surprise, the doctor came to see me. He sat at my bedside for a while, assuring me that, despite the pain and discomfort, I would be all right. He also said that had I waited a bit longer (as if I had had control over that), I would have developed blood poisoning which would probably have been resistant to whatever treatment was available. His visits continued for several evenings. He never stayed long, but he carefully examined my legs and gently soothed my fears. I knew that during his years at the front he had seen a great deal that was far worse than my condition, and that there must have been many times when he felt totally helpless in the face of suffering and death. And clearly I was on the mend and did not require his medical skills any longer. Perhaps he found comfort in his ability to be a physician in the full sense of the word once more; to tend to the patient as a person, even in the absence of a grave physical threat. It was 'time out' from the brutality and carnage of the battlefield. If my happiness at seeing him meant as much to him as his visits meant to me, it may have helped him to recapture the true vocation of a healer. My pain and his kindness are forever intertwined in my memory. I still recall his presence and how comforted I felt, night after night, that he had come to see me. I have no memory of our conversations, or of our parting. Perhaps one day he just did not come, and I knew that much as I missed him, I was well again.

**** *young man*

The young man appeared out of nowhere. If my sister did not remember him, I might believe that he is but a figment of my imagination. Despite a vivid pictorial memory of the first time I saw him, the encounter has a dream-like quality. He was exceedingly handsome – tall and fair, in his late twenties or early thirties. To my teenage eyes he appeared godlike – untouched by war, suffering or deprivation. Why he approached me, an unremarkable scrawny girl with a serious face, sad eyes and ugly sores on her legs, I do not know. He asked me my name (I believe it was the first time in almost a year that I identified myself with my real name) and where I lived. We must have talked for a while, although I have no recollection of anything we may have said to each other during that first conversation, nor of the language in which we communicated. Was it Slovak, Hungarian, German, or did I speak Slovak and he another Slavic language which I could understand? The language he used might have been a clue to his nationality, but in the multilingual environment of central Europe, that would not necessarily be the case. All I remember is that, from the first time I saw him, I was hopelessly smitten.

My joy was boundless when, in the evening, he appeared at our door, his arms laden with food we could only have dreamt of. He did not introduce himself, nor did he say why he came or explain how he managed to gather the gifts he offered us. When he and I went out for a walk I told him about our family and our war experiences. He revealed nothing about himself. I held my tongue, clutched his hand, and listened to my heart. His presence, for me pure magic, illuminated our family existence for several days. Always unannounced, he came bearing gifts, clearly delighted by our amazement at the bounty which he deposited in our kitchen. He took me for a ride in his car (it may have been a military vehicle) and I fell deeply in love. I knew nothing about his origins or his destination. In a scarred and mutilated world, he seemed to have come from another planet – a place where there was neither war nor deprivation. I do not remember asking questions. Perhaps I did not want to know that he was just an ordinary mortal whose life, too, had been touched by suffering and death; or I was afraid to hear that our time together was to end shortly. He disappeared as suddenly as he appeared, with no warnings and no goodbyes. To this day he has remained for me a luminous, quasi-mythical presence; an apparition without wounds, untouched by ugliness or suffering. Dropping unexpectedly into our midst, he helped awaken in me the belief that life might have another side – where generosity, beauty and abundance were the norm. He was the first man I fell in love with. Had I had a more ordinary life, my first love would probably have been an adolescent schoolboy. Instead, my first love was remarkable for his mysterious origins, his maturity, his physical beauty, and his concern for my well being. I felt bereft, but neither surprised nor betrayed, when he disappeared. I knew right from the start that one day I would wait and he would not come. He gave so much, and asked for nothing in return.

The elderly woman ****

When my father left for Košice shortly after we moved from the Črmáň back into Nitra, we had more living space than we needed, or were allowed to have. We shared the spare room in our apartment with an elderly woman whom we did not know. After years in a concentration camp, she had returned to Slovakia in the hope of finding at least some surviving members of her family. But her efforts were unrewarded and she could find no traces, nor pick up rumours, leading to a familiar and loved face. Her despair was profound and total. Skeletal in appearance, she talked little, ate even less, and walked with the gait of a sleepwalker, barely conscious of her surroundings. She was a constant reminder of the deep divide between those very few of us who, regardless of the hardships we endured, had spent some part of the war in hiding and who emerged as a family, and those who had been sent to concentration camps and came back alone. And then came the moment when she, the most pitiful of victims, saved us.

Since Slovakia was considered a conquered country that had fought on the side of the enemy, rather than a country liberated from German occupation (as the Czech and Moravian parts of Czechoslovakia were seen), few restraints were imposed on the occupying Russian soldiers. They looted and raped at will, making no distinctions between friends and foes. Rumour had it that the Soviet Army, bitter at what it considered the betrayal by fellow Slavs who had fought against them alongside the German forces, sent some of their most degraded and worst trained troops to occupy Slovakia. Many of them were battle weary, ignorant, brutal and merciless. Locks and chains on the doors did not deter them. Often drunk and aroused, they had the strength, and the will, to break through any homemade barriers to entry. They were neither restrained from committing crimes on civilians, nor were they punished when charges were brought against them. Rape was not a military weapon, as it has become in more recent conflicts, to be used to intimidate, humiliate or subjugate the civilian population. These soldiers looked at rape as a trophy they earned for their war service.

One evening, shortly after our move back to Nitra, we heard an ominous knock on our door. Before we had a chance to think about escape or make a feeble attempt at hiding, we were confronted by several Russian soldiers, in various stages of inebriation. Their intentions were clear. They wanted young girls, and Vlasta, Greta and I were just about the right age. We froze in terror. Did we survive the war only to be destroyed by our liberators? We knew instinctively that reasoning or pleading would only arouse them more, and that any attempt to resist would enrage them. Like many traumatic events, the initial confrontation is a blur in my memory. I can recall the feelings, but not the facts. And then out of nowhere, before any physical contact occurred, the ghost-like figure of our tenant, Pani Trattnerová, appeared in the room, with what turned out to be a Bible in her hand. God only knows where and how she found it, or how, in her confused state, she even recognized that it was a 'holy' book. Like a demented fury she circled around the soldiers, pointing to the Bible and repeating, as if it were an incantation, '*Ivrity, Ivrity*' (Hebrews, Hebrews). Creating a momentary disturbance, she could have been ignored, shot, thrown out of the window, or shoved aside. While most of the soldiers paid no attention to her, one of them, who seemed to be in charge, took the Bible from her and started leafing through it. I do not know whether he recognized the book he was holding in his hands, and even if he did, whether it meant anything to him or evoked distant memories of another time and another life. Whatever his reasons, abruptly, and with great authority, he ordered the soldiers out of the apartment. Even in their drunken state, they obeyed. As the doors closed behind them we knew that we had had a narrow escape and, at best, a temporary reprieve. We were terrified that the same soldiers, without their commander, would return some other night and exact vengeance, or that they might send their comrades to accomplish what they themselves had failed to do. We knew we would not be saved twice. We also knew that Pani Trattnerová would never be able to perform the miracle a second time. After the soldiers left, she withdrew into her shell and continued her somnambulant existence.

Once again, we needed help. Pán Laco, our Črmáň neighbour, knew two people with connections to the local mental institutions, Pani Helena Slabejová and Dr. Závodny, and he asked them to arrange for Vlasta, Greta, my sister (who was then only ten), and me to be admitted to the hospital for observation, under the pretext that all four of us seemed to be suffering from a mental disorder brought on by our war experiences. Ironically, while most of the city hospitals were crowded, there were empty beds in the asylum. Thus, we moved out of a world that had gone mad for six years, and found ourselves in an institution where the mad were supposedly locked up and separated from the rest of society. While incarcerated, we engaged in a certain amount of play acting, which we quite enjoyed – pretending we had terrible headaches, tics, and lapses of memory. Acting our parts made us feel that we were not inmates; that our roles were part of a theatre production we had been asked to stage. We imagined that we could leave at any time – mind and body intact. That was our secret and differentiated us from the others, who seemed to have little control over their thoughts and actions. We were play-acting again, but this time our 'secret' was that we were sane and that we were confined for our physical safety.

There was one phrase, '*Nebodske Radio*' (heavenly radio), which, for reasons we could not fathom, gave us great power on our ward. When we uttered the two words one of the inmates went wild, and in no time the whole floor was in an uproar. I cannot even guess how we came upon that phrase, or why it was so powerful. But both Vlasta and I remember clearly that with those two words we could conjure up an atmosphere of utter madness and chaos whenever we thought it was necessary to deflect attention from ourselves. So in a sense we were stage managers and actors, although we were not really free to leave when the play was done. The world outside was dangerous.

We stayed in the mental institution for several weeks, until my father came to pick us up for our move to Košice. We were relieved to leave the city in which we had lived the last terrible months of the war and its bitter aftermath. Although apprehensive about the future, we looked forward to returning to some form of normal existence. Even the prospect of taking entrance exams for the gymnasium, attending school with regular schedules and daily homework, was exciting. We did not know then that in about three years' time we would be on the road again. We yearned for permanence and a life that pointed toward a future.

8 Three Transitional Years: Fragments

A few years ago, I came across three photographs taken in 1948 – probably in early autumn, a couple of months before we left Košice for America. One was of two young girls, identified on the back as Nuša and Eva. (Eva was perhaps the most popular name for girls in Czechoslovakia and Hungary in the 1930s, and I had several friends with whom I shared the name.) Another was of Eva alone and the third was of Eva and me. The picture of the two friends together bears the inscription on the back 'To a dear friend, to remember V-B, Nuša and Eva'; the picture of Eva by herself carries the inscription 'Dedicated to Evička, with eternal friendship, Eva'. The picture of me and Eva is inscribed by Eva, 'To dear Evička for beautiful memories of our young years and our common experiences'. I wonder what unfulfilled promises I made on their copies of the same pictures. In these photographs all three of us look young, vulnerable, full of dreams and expectations. I have tried very hard to bring the pictures to life – to remember who Eva and Nuša were, how we became friends, how we spent our time together, what silly dreams we shared and what secrets we might have exchanged. But nothing, absolutely nothing, comes back to me. Reference to V-B must mean that we were schoolmates in Grade V-B and attended the same Gymnasium. On my return visit to the Girls' Gymnasium in Košice in the summer of 1993, I hoped to recapture some scenes from the three years I spent there, and find a clue to the identity of the two girls, Eva and Nuša, who swore eternal friendship to me. But my mind was totally blank then, as it is now. As I walked up and down the halls and peered into classrooms I could not activate even the faintest recollection of my friends and of our youthful devotion to each other. Nothing stirred in the recesses of memory. Forgetting hardship and suffering is a powerful weapon in the service of life. But why forget affection, loyalty, common pursuits? Eva and Nuša may have

91

forgotten me long ago, but I need to hold on to the fact that they existed and that we were friends. It is reassuring to know that our war experiences did not render me incapable of forming strong relationships with people who had not shared our suffering and who had lived on the other side of the divide. It is equally reassuring to know that there were people on that other side of the divide who were glad that I survived the war and who became my friends. I feel both sad and guilty about forgetting them.

Forgetting Nuša and Eva are not isolated lapses of memory about events that took place between our arrival in Košice in the late summer of 1945, and our departure a little over three years later. I have almost total amnesia, with some striking exceptions, about that period. It is easy to understand the need to repress the traumatic events that occurred during the war years; it is more difficult to grasp the significance of forgetting so many important chapters from our lives after the liberation. By then I was no longer a child, and the life I led, after the first few months, had order, structure and a measure of security. Perhaps I was so keen to forget the past that I unwittingly continued to keep the brain's storage bins marked 'personal life events' closed. Or perhaps, just like a child learning to walk, I concentrated so powerfully on the next steps I had to take that I neglected to hold on to the events as they passed by. Or possibly, by coming to America, we began life over again in such a radically different environment that the new experiences, instead of building on the old ones, buried them. Even if there is some truth in these speculations, they do not account for the fact that both my siblings, one younger and the other one older, remember so much more than I do. This lack of personal recollections is all the more puzzling since, in my studies as well as in my professional life, I have been greatly aided by a very good memory, both in my ability to store factual information and in making connections between ideas and events that are seemingly unrelated.

While I do not have many memories of our years in Košice, I assume that I was not unhappy and that I settled into my own adolescent routine. I remember moments of rebellion against my parents' expectations of proper behaviour and religious observance: surely a sign of a well-adjusted teenager! I know with certainty that when, in the autumn of 1948, my father decided that we had to leave Czechoslovakia, I objected vociferously. By then I had my future planned out. In less than a year I would have caught up with all the schooling I had missed during the war and would have started medical studies in Prague. I did well in school, enjoyed both the learning and the camaraderie with my schoolmates, and looked forward to the independence that would come once I left home. Normal life was just beyond the horizon. But the horizon kept receding.

The fragments I remember about our lives, and the lives of Teta and Vlasta, do not add up to a narrative. I have filled out some of the interstices with information from Vlasta and my siblings, particulary about the three years we spent in Košice, but also about events after 1948, when we parted from Teta and Vlasta to start a new life – my mother, my siblings and I in America and my father in Israel.

Teta and Vlasta never left Košice, and so, in a sense, the story I have to tell about them temporarily ends here – to be picked up again over 50 years later when Vlasta came to visit us in America. Shortly after our arrival from Nitra, Teta took a job as a bookkeeper and Vlasta attended school until the age of eighteen. I believe that we saw each other with some frequency, and I remember occasional visits, but I have no recollection of how, after months of living together in close quarters, we dealt with the separation. Did it feel natural, or artificial? Did both families try to create a new life for themselves? My parents became very involved in Jewish and Zionist affairs, and Teta, a young woman just thirty years old, was ready to establish herself in Košice. In 1953, after years of courtship, Teta married Robert Göblov, a baker. We referred to him as 'Robi Bácsi', Hungarian for 'Uncle Robi'. They were happy together. Despite the difficult war years, Teta continued to be an optimistic and fun loving person. She enjoyed cooking, needlework (when Vlasta came to America she brought me table coverings embroidered by her mother), trips to the countryside, movies and, above all, she loved people. She was a devoted wife and mother and she has remained for me, over all these years, the unforgettable 'Teta'. The very ordinariness of her life belied the heroism of her soul and the goodness of her heart. Her happiness was cut short in 1961, when Robi Bácsi suffered his first stroke. Cared for by Teta and Vlasta in their house on Muškatova ulica 36, he died in 1976. Measured in material terms, their lives were modest; measured in terms of love and devotion, they were as rich as royalty. I have a small picture of the three of them sitting in their living room in 1967. Crowded around a table, they are surrounded by plants, baskets, Slovak folk ornaments on the walls and three birds in a bird cage. Teta and Robi Bácsi are looking at each other with the eyes of newlyweds; Vlasta, then in her early thirties, is sitting next to her mother, smiling and content. Formal portraits may lie – snapshots seldom do.

Teta and Vlasta mourned the passing of Robi Bácsi and kept his memory alive. After his death, the tone of Teta's letters to me changed. She dwelt more on the past than on the future, and wrote about their happy lives together rather than about the things she might do next. Yet she did not complain or rail against fate, and never asked me for anything except for my freely given love. She and Vlasta moved to a smaller apartment on Československa Armády 27 in Nove Mesto, a sprawling neighbourhood on the outskirts of Košice, where Vlasta still lives. Teta survived Robi Bácsi by six years. She died on 4 December 1982, a month before her 68th birthday. She is buried next to him at the Košice cemetery.

****

Things were different for my family. In September of 1945, my brother and I took entrance exams to determine the appropriate grade level at which we should enter the local Gymnasium. For the first four and a half years of the war, from the beginning of 1939 until the fall of 1944, we attended school only sporadically (I learned the multiplication tables in Hungarian in the Tolcsva village school) and then, in the last year, not at all. Not surprisingly, we got abysmal results on our qualifying exams. Our vast experience of life did not translate into academic excellence. Both my brother and I started in grades several levels below what would have been age appropriate. We studied hard, I with more diligence than he, and from time to time we skipped grades. By the time we left in the fall of 1948, my brother and I were within a year, or at most a year and a half, of graduation

from the Gymnasium. We both finished our secondary schooling at night at McKinley High School in Washington, D.C.

I believe that it was in the early spring of 1948, when the communists overthrew the democratically elected government of
Eduard Beneš, that all parochial schools, from Kindergarten to
the last grades of Gymnasium, were abolished and their teach-
ers, mostly nuns, were transferred to public schools.
Notwithstanding their long black robes, their covered heads,
their large wooden crucifixes and their deeply religious observances, which gave them exemption from eating with us during
the midday meals, they taught us physics, algebra, Latin and
civics. Ironically, religion, still a required subject for all students
in the Gymnasium, was not taught by the nuns, but by local
parish priests. Formal religious instruction was in Catholicism.
Children of other religions were excused from these classes but
had to provide proof that they received religious instruction
through their own churches or synagogues. I managed to get a
double dose of religious instruction: from the Jewish school I
attended in the afternoons, and from the Catholic priest who
taught in the Gymnasium, whose classes I voluntarily attended.
In very different ways, both religions had played an important
part in our lives and I wanted to know more about them. One
was at the core of our identity, the other was a significant source
of our persecutions.

The nuns were not pleased to be in our school, nor were we
pleased by the prospect of their presence. We expected them to
be rigid, humourless, strict disciplinarians and tough graders.
We were warned that they would not tolerate teenage pranks or
vulgar jokes, and that even the smallest transgression would be
followed swiftly by punishment in this world, and who knows
by what else in the world to come.

I shared the apprehensions of my classmates, and then I had
some of my own. Growing up with Father Tiso as the head of
the Slovak Republic during the war, I had ample reason to look
at the Catholic religion in general, and at those who had dedicated their lives to the Church in particular, as sworn enemies of
the Jews. In the beginning, I was not prepared to make fine distinctions – separating the teachings of the Church from the historical institutions which professed them, or specific individuals
from the collective of which they were members. The crucifix

belonged to our historical enemy who had now infiltrated my classroom. My experiences during the last year in the Gymnasium proved my apprehensions groundless and taught me important lessons about love and forgiveness which I have not forgotten. In ways that I do not understand completely, they provided a transition between my wounded war time existence and my new life in America. And so, in a way, parts of this chapter are also about 'good beyond evil'.

One teacher in particular, Sestra Smutná (Sister Sad), who taught science and mathematics, took a great interest in me. Without ever talking to her about it, I sensed that her attachment to me was in some way related to my being a Jewish child who had survived the war. She was attentive, gentle, kind and encouraging, making it clear that she expected great things of me – without pressuring me or making demands. Whenever her strict religious schedule allowed it she stayed after school to help me get ahead and to prepare me to skip a grade. It was not simply that she devoted extra time to tutor me in difficult subjects that had to be learned sequentially – or at least that is not how I experienced it. It was as if by reviewing the textbook lessons with me, she was performing an act of penance, asking for forgiveness, making amends for the persecution and losses I had suffered. She wanted me to succeed, not only in a worldly, but also in a moral, sense, as if my success could, in a very small way, right a very big wrong in which her Church was complicit. Her acts foreshadowed, in a simple and concrete way, the formal apologies to the Jewish people expressed by the Church, the Pope and the Bishops from many countries in the last years of the twentieth century. Whatever difference these statements of contrition may make in the future relations between the Church and the Jews, and whatever real or perceived inadequacies they may contain, the acts of Sestra Smutná had an immediate and powerful effect. I have two vivid memories of Sestra Smutná. The first is of a class outing, the high point of the academic year, for which the school supplied food and beverages. After a morning of running around and playing games, we were ravenous and attacked our picnic baskets with great gusto. When I saw Sestra Smutná sitting with us, touching neither food nor drink, I lost all desire to eat. I turned away from my friends and tried to engage her in conversation. While the others ate, we talked.

love

The substance of our conversation is now long forgotten, but not the love that infused it. I did not even realize how exceptional our relationship was until my classmates asked me whether Sestra Smutná was trying to convert me. They teased that a nun's habits would suit my sombre face. What a catch I would be. A soul snatched from the claws of the devil and delivered to God would surely earn her extra credit in eternity! The truth, I remain convinced to this day, was the opposite. She loved me because I was a Jewish child who survived, not because I was a damned soul she wanted to convert.

While the first memory is located on a secular playing field, the location of the second one is the convent where Sestra Smutná lived with other nuns in strict seclusion. A friend and I had baked a cake in our home economics class, and we were encouraged by our teacher to take it home and share it with our families. Instead of dividing it between us, I suggested that we take it to Sestra Smutná. My friend, worldlier than I, thought this was a splendid idea, but insisted that I deliver it by myself. Even today, despite the serious memory lapses I so often experience, I see with utmost clarity the large, iron gate of the convent. The entrance was locked. To gain admittance I had to pull on a heavy chain several times, with ever increasing apprehension, to activate a bell (to me it sounded more like an alarm) on the inside. Finally, the door opened, just a crack. An old nun, peering through a small aperture asked, without any encouragement or curiosity, what I wanted. In that instant I knew with absolute certainty that I had done something very inappropriate and, even more important, that I had transgressed a powerful prohibition the nature of which was not yet clear to me. The best I could do was to stammer that my friend and I had baked a cake in our home economics class that we wanted to give to our teacher, Sestra Smutná. How I wished for the presence of my fellow baker to corroborate my story, to share my embarrassment and to give me courage! After what seemed hours of waiting at the front entrance, the old nun returned and asked that I follow her. Behind an iron grid, at the end of a large, dark room, stood Sestra Smutná. I had one powerful wish: that the earth would open and swallow me. That, of course, did not happen. Instead, I walked up to where she stood behind a partition. Calm, gentle and smiling, she told me that the rules of her Order forbid any nun to accept a gift, no matter how trifling and well intentioned. I was prepared to leave, cake in hand, when she added that she was very happy that I brought the cake and that, if I agreed, she would take it and share it with the other nuns at their communal meal. Relieved and eager to leave the convent as soon as possible, I moved forward to hand her the cake, only to discover that the opening in the partition was too small for the cake to slip through. The old nun appeared again at my side, took the cake from me and, without uttering a word or making the slightest attempt to put me at ease, escorted me to the door through which I had entered. Sestra Smutná never mentioned the incident to me, and I was too embarrassed to explain or apologize. What I never doubted was that she understood the nature of my offering and was touched by it. I also knew that it must have been difficult for her to persuade the older nuns of her Order that it was more important to accept the cake than it was to follow the letter of their rules. I wonder whether she told them that the bearer of the gift was a Jewish girl.

I was powerfully reminded of this incident many years later, in the early 1980s, when the mother of a student to whom I had been helpful during her recovery from a serious car accident wanted to show her gratitude by presenting me with a silver pen. I understood the generosity of the gesture, but I had a firm rule of accepting only trifles or things that were edible and could be shared by the staff in the office of the Dean of the College. In the awkward silence that followed her gesture, the spirit of Sestra Smutná unexpectedly came to my rescue. Remembering how rebuffed and embarrassed I felt holding the cake in my hand, I suggested to the mother that she keep the pen until her daughter's graduation, and if at that time she still felt that she wanted me to have it, I would gratefully accept it. Three years passed and I completely forgot the incident. On the day of her daughter's graduation, in the midst of family celebrations and a great deal of institutional pomp and ceremony, she stopped by my office and handed me a small, splendidly wrapped package. I knew instantly that it was the pen, which she had kept, and perhaps even occasionally polished, for over three years. It remains one of my prized possessions and when I use it I think both of the student, who is now a successful physician, and of Sestra Smutná, who, if there are angels, dwells among them.

****

Although I did not know it at the time, the same communist coup d'état, in February 1948, that brought Sestra Smutná to our Gymnasium, also shattered any illusions my parents may have had about rebuilding our lives in Košice. The take-over was the culmination of a gradual process of political manoeuvring and, in hindsight, may have been inevitable. The Czechoslovak Government in exile had included in its ranks active and old time members of the Communist party, as well as committed liberals and democrats. Much of the organized opposition to German occupation, including the uprising in Banská Bystrica in the fall of 1944, was spearheaded by communists, from both within and outside the country. Hence, while the government of Eduard Beneš returned from London to Prague triumphantly in May 1945 with a mandate to reunite the Czech and Slovak lands and to create a democratic state, more or less geographically and historically continuous with pre-war Czechoslovakia, the coalition between those members of his government in exile who favoured restoring a democratic government and those who believed in Soviet style Communism was fragile from the very beginning. In the June 1946 parliamentary elections the Communist Party led in Bohemia and Moravia, while the democratic party won a majority in Slovakia. Klement Gottwald, chairman of the Czechoslovak Communist Party, was asked to form a government, while Eduard Beneš remained President and Jan Masaryk, the son of the first President of Czechoslovakia, Thomáš Garrigue Masaryk, served as Foreign Minister. On 10 March 1948, shortly after the communist coup, when the non-communist cabinet members resigned in protest against the Communist Party's attempts to take control of the police, Jan Masaryk committed suicide (we were convinced that he was thrown out of the window – defenestration was the term we used). Several months later, in June 1948, President Beneš resigned and two hard line communists, Klement Gottwald and Antonin Zapotocky, became President and Prime Minister respectively.

The departure of both Masaryk and Beneš from the government signalled the end of the short lived revival of a democratic Czechoslovakia. It was at this point that it became clear to my parents that the Czechoslovak state we had known before the war would not be rebuilt in the foreseeable future. Even under the most favourable political circumstances, it would have taken decades to re-establish a thriving Jewish community in Czechoslovakia. With the destruction of democratic institutions and the growing presence of a new form of totalitarianism, that hope became an impossible dream. Ominous clouds were gathering rapidly, not only in Czechoslovakia, but in all of eastern Europe. My parents assessed the risks and decided to uproot once more. While, at the beginning, the Jews were not singled out for especially harsh treatment, it was only a matter of time before the forces of anti-Semitism, anti-Zionism, totalitarianism and anti-bourgeois resentment would merge into an ideology that would make Jews targets of hatred and persecutions once more.

While most human traits are the result of millions of years of evolution, coupled with thousands of years of experience, our senses for detecting danger were honed during the six years of the war. Or perhaps we just skipped millennia to reconnect with our animal ancestors, who had such an acute capacity to detect danger in their surroundings. In any case, our parents saw the handwriting on the wall, and three years after we had settled in Košice we were on the move again.

Our preparations for departure started in the summer of 1948. I was the first to be sent out of the country under a pretext I no longer remember. I know that I had a one way ticket to England, with clearly no expectation that I would return. During the stopover in Prague with my mother, who was accompanying me part of the way and was to stay with me until I boarded the train for London, we received an urgent call from my father to return to Košice immediately. He had just heard that our relatives in America had succeeded in securing an immigration visa for my mother, who was a German national, and that she would be allowed to bring her children if they were under the age of 21. It is surely ironic that we came to the United States on the German quota. Given the exclusion of Germans with a Nazi past from eligibility for immigration to North America (unless, of course, they were world class scientists), the quota remained unfilled three years after the war, and we were eligible. My father, who was a Czechoslovak national, would not be allowed to join us. And so, once again, our choice was to separate or to face an uncertain and dangerous future together. Caution prevailed. My mother and her three children (aged twelve, seventeen and eighteen) arrived in the United States on 2 November 1948. My father left for Israel in the spring of 1949.

It was thus from a safe distance that we watched the destruction of a democratic Czechoslovakia for the second time, again coupled with an attack on the now pitifully decimated Jewish communities. Much of the anti-Semitic rhetoric of the war years resurfaced, especially during the trials of Slánský and his 13 colleagues, 11 of whom were Jews, all of them dedicated communists, which took place between 1951 and 1952. As the prosecution developed its case against these former high ranking members of the Communist Party, anti-Semitic rhetoric again gained legal status in the Czechoslovak law courts. The charges read, in part:

> These traitors against the Czechoslovak people...infiltrated into important positions in the government and party, disguised and dangerous enemies of the Czechoslovakian people's democracy: Trotskyists, Zionists, bourgeois nationalists, col-laborationists, capitalists...When the nation raised its voice against Zionism...(the accused) cried 'anti-Semitism' in order to cover the help they were giving the class interests of the Jewish bourgeoisie and their ties with the imperialists through world Zionism. (From Mir Cotic, *The Prague Trial*, Herzl Press, New York, 1987)

The trial ended with the same judicial travesty that marked it from the beginning. With total disregard for an independent court, the sentences for all the defendants were determined by the President of the Republic, Clement Gottwald, with the concurrence of Soviet advisers. The decision of the 'court' was announced by the presiding judge, Dr Jaroslav Novak. As in true Kafkaland, all those condemned to death (except for Slánský) used established judicial procedures and appealed for clemency to the President of the Republic. Their requests were denied. On 4 December 1952, less than 13 months after the arrest of Slánský, the sentences were carried out.

101

In 1953, five years after our arrival, my mother, sister and I became citizens of the United States. I passed my citizenship exam with flying colours, but was stumped at the end when I was asked to rank, on a scale of evil, the Nazi and Communist regimes under which I had lived. I answered truthfully, that for me there was no comparison, since a decent human being could believe in the ideals of the Communist Party, no matter how twisted they became in reality, while that was not possible in the case of the Nazis, where the ideology was as evil as the reality which embodied it. My momentary fear, that perhaps I would be denied citizenship, has to be understood in the context of the Cold War atmosphere. My brother, in recognition of his military service with the United States Air Force during the Korean War, had received his citizenship the year before. Our 'Americanization' was now official. But our ties with Czechoslovakia were not completely severed, although it took us close to 50 years to pick up our 'unfinished business'.

9 Reunion

Leaving Košice for America was difficult. Once again, we had to uproot ourselves from familiar surroundings and take a journey into the unknown. I had conflicting images of America – as the land of milk and honey, the place where many succeeded and a few failed, the home to countless European immigrants, the refuge of crooks and criminals, the country that helped save Europe from Nazi domination, the melting pot of the world, the land of cowboys and Indians. The America of my imagination was vast, rich, powerful, exotic and impersonal. My facts were meagre. They were gathered from news broadcasts, from the content of occasional food packages we received from the American Joint Distribution Committee, from relatives who had left Europe before it was too late, and from stories about the 'wild west' my brother and I read after the war. (The sum total of my knowledge about the American Civil War and slavery came from *Gone with the Wind*, which I read in Hungarian!) What I knew with certainty was that I was leaving the world of my childhood for good. What I did not know, and could not have known, was that I would never see Teta again, or that both Vlasta and I would be in advanced middle age before we were reunited. I do not remember what promises we made to each other when we parted, although I am sure we pretended that our separation was only temporary. It was easier that way.

During our first few years in America we led a typical immigrant life, filled with many struggles and much hope. While I could not erase the past, I was quite certain that I could transcend it. With the optimism that continues to be characteristic of every new wave of immigrants, I believed that it was in my power to shape my life and to earn a share in the American dream. My eyes were fixed on the future. Czechoslovakia was no longer my homeland, but a graveyard, with not even markers or stones for family and friends. The detachment from the country in which I spent most of my first seventeen years was made easier by the fact that my memories of the past were fragmented and disjointed. I seldom spoke Slovak and after the spring of 1949, when my father left for Israel, I took little interest in the political events of Czechoslovakia. I never thought of myself as a Slovak-American. The dominant metaphor of the time was the 'melting pot', rather than the 'hyphen'; 'Americanization', rather than 'identity politics'.

Although it was easy to repress the past, I could not forget Teta and Vlasta. Much as I was racing toward the future, I carried within me the sense that there was some 'unfinished business' in my childhood that needed to be attended to – not exorcised on a psychiatric couch, but acted on in real life. For years I had made faithful, but in retrospect, quite feeble and inadequate attempts to keep in touch with Teta and Vlasta. Around Christmas time each year I sent them an account of our lives in America – in increasingly more pitiful Slovak, until Teta, shortly before her death, was moved to send me an English-Slovak dictionary – and enclosed modest sums of money or gift certificates that could be exchanged in the 'dollar' stores reserved for diplomats. Teta's letters were cheerful while Robi Bácsi was alive, and even as their tone became more sombre after his death, they remained unfailingly loving, informative, and full of questions about our lives. I regret deeply that often she had to wait a full year for an answer. And yet I know that I never ceased to love her, and that she loved me in return.

When Teta died in 1982, and Vlasta took over as the family correspondent, I knew with absolute certainty, and great sorrow, that I had failed Teta in important, human ways. If there is a way of making amends to the dead, it can only be done by trying to do better for the living. I was determined not to fail Vlasta, but it took me almost a decade to act on my resolve. Although I made several half hearted attempts to visit her, I was too easily discouraged by the morose responses from the Czechoslovak travel bureau, first in Paris, where we lived for a year and where we spent many summers, and then in New York. I wanted to see Vlasta, but I was not ready to go back. Finally, in the winter of 1991, I knew that I did not want to wait any longer and we invited her to visit us during the Christmas holidays.

As soon as I put her airline tickets in the mail, I became pre-occupied with our reunion. Would we recognize each other when we first met in a crowded airline terminal? Would we like each other? Would we be able to recapture the intimacy we shared during the war, based on danger, hunger, fear and cunning? Would we be able to communicate with ease, or would linguistic and cultural barriers make our efforts halting and half-hearted? Would she be jealous of my materially comfortable and intellectually stimulating surroundings, and would I feel guilty about her difficult and circumscribed life? Would there be too many regrets and too little joy? Would her presence awaken in both of us painful memories and suppressed fears? Would we be strangers, uncomfortable with each other? Would the visit drive a wedge into our fragile relationship? I had many questions, but no answers and no certainties.

Then the unexpected happened. The day before Vlasta's arrival in New York I came down with a severe case of flu. I did not know then that it would hang on for weeks, but I did know with absolute certainty that I would never make it to the airport, even stretched out in the back of the car. Was this a bad omen – a sign that one should not attempt to recapture the past – especially one fraught with so much loss and suffering? Was I affected with a metaphysical or psychological illness (I did think of *Death in Venice!*) or had I succumbed to an ordinary virus? My fever was real, but was I somehow responsible for it? Was I, once again, letting Vlasta down? But Vlasta was on her way and it was too late for these questions. Fretting in bed was self-indulgent and hardly provided a plan of action. What we needed was a practical solution. The obvious answer was to send a limousine, but we were concerned that Vlasta might be reluctant to get into a car with a total stranger, with whom she could hardly communicate, and set out for the two-hour trip from Kennedy airport to Princeton. How many gangster movies would flash through her mind if, instead of seeing me, she were approached by a driver whom she could barely understand and whom she had no reason to expect? My husband, who had only seen a small snapshot of Vlasta when she was in her early thirties, volunteered to go to the airport by himself, armed with a sign saying VLASTA KRESCANKOVÁ. In my feverish and over-wrought state, the five-hour wait between the time he left and

105

his expected return seemed interminable. Did he get to the airport on time? Would they find each other? How would they communicate? What will Vlasta think when she does not see me at the airport? My exaggerated fears were undoubtedly connected with the state of my shivering body, but may also have been re-enactments of the states of terror and helplessness that were so familiar to all of us during our years of hiding.

When Vlasta and my husband walked through the door, my fears, doubts and anxieties disappeared instantaneously. It was clear that they had not only found each other at the airport without undue delay, but also immediately liked each other and quickly and cleverly devised ways to communicate – he in half-remembered Russian, she in broken English. In a flash I knew that I was meeting my friend of long ago. The intervening years had put lines on our faces, very different life experiences into the 'knapsacks' we carried on our backs, but they had not erected barriers between us.

Vlasta's two giant suitcases of pre-war vintage were back-breakingly heavy, though they contained hardly any personal items and only a modest wardrobe of a few skirts and blouses that would have easily fit into an overnight case. The remaining spaces were filled with presents that must have taken her months to assemble at a cost equivalent to her annual salary. There was something for every member of the family – crystal vases, jewellery, books, souvenirs, brandy, chocolates, dolls dressed in national costumes, table coverings embroidered by Teta, travel books about Slovakia, and so on. She was so happy emptying her suitcases, holding up each item and asking, tentatively yet hopefully, *'Páči sa ty?'* (Do you like it?) that I did not have the heart to show her my consternation. I knew how small her income was, and how few luxuries she could afford. But why should I have been surprised that the young child, who so cheerfully, and without complaints, shared a life of hardship and danger with us, would grow into a woman whose greatest pleasure was to bring gifts to her old friends?

The piles of presents on the floor served as material conduits to the life stories of our family members. Before we could decide which present went to whom, I thought she should know something about the intended recipients. Unlike Sheherezade, who told one story a night over 101 nights, I tried to compress 43

years of our lives into one long night. In halting Slovak, gener-
ously supplemented by body language and with occasional help
from the English-Slovak dictionary Teta had sent to me more
than ten years earlier, I sifted through my memories to recall
events in our four-decade-long journey that would help Vlasta
make the connection between the family she said goodbye to in
October 1948, and the one she would now encounter. From my
annual letters, first to her mother and then to her, she was familiar with the broad outlines of what had become of us, but what
she knew was abstract, fragmented and lifeless.

I started at the beginning. I told her about our cramped
existence in a small rented apartment above a dry goods store on
a commercial street in Washington, D.C., considerably less
spacious than our post-war apartment in Košice, and I described
to her our gradual transformation from eastern European
refugees to American citizens. By sharing the memories with
her, I was able to recall with considerable clarity the motley crew
of students, young and old, simple and well educated, who had
gathered from all corners of the earth in the 'Americanization
School' (how quaint the term sounds today!), which all of us
attended to learn English as well as the rudiments of American
culture and mores. The efforts of our teacher, Mrs. Vaša, who
was the widow of a Czech general, were supplemented, especially for my brother and me, by what we learned from
frequenting the movie house across the street from our apartment. Mrs. Vaša taught us to read, write and speak English
grammatically and fluently. The movies taught us to dream and
to fantasize in English and may have given us some pointers
about sex and love. I told Vlasta, who over the years had made
half-hearted attempts to learn English, that had she come with
us she would have enjoyed at least part of the process. But just
as I could not imagine what would have become of us had we
stayed in Slovakia, I could not conjure up a picture of an
'Americanized' Vlasta. And yet we talked with an ease and a love
that belied our very different life experiences.

Vlasta had many questions about my mother, whom she
called '*mamička*', the diminutive for 'mother' in Slovak. What
she recalled most vividly about her were her scrupulous religious observances, even while we were in hiding, and her
refusal to touch non-kosher meat or break the laws of the

Sabbath. She was, therefore, not surprised when I told her that shortly after our arrival in America my mother became a Hebrew teacher, and that she held that position until her retirement in her early seventies. She was pleased to hear that my mother, who had never held a job before, derived much satisfaction from her teaching, and that at the end of her career she received the Lion of Judah award for her contribution to Jewish education. Remembering my mother as a relatively young woman, about eight years older than Teta, whose life had centred around her family and her community, Vlasta also understood that, later on in life, her greatest satisfaction came from the love and loyalty of generations of her students who have continued to keep in touch with her. Vlasta thought hard before she selected from among the presents she brought the books and jewellery she wanted *mamička* to have.

The picture Vlasta carried of my sister was of a chubby thirteen-year-old with long, dark, curly hair and a sunny disposition. She now had to readjust her image to encompass a middle aged married woman with two children and two grandchildren. I fast forwarded a few years and started her story with her graduation from Brooklyn College and her marriage in Israel. I then described, as briefly as I could, my sister's life-long career as a Hebrew teacher and her innovative teaching of Judaism to both children and adults. I told her about the Holocaust curriculum she devised for her classes, and her efforts to make the students active participants in a period of history so distant from their own experiences. The highlight of the school year was the annual production of a play about the Holocaust, researched, written, produced and performed by her students. I told her that my sister often talked to her classes about our lives with Teta and her, emphasizing that even when the world was dominated by evil, there were points of bright light. Vlasta found it hard to believe that she and her mother had a palpable presence in an American classroom filled with children whose parents were born after the war. But, I pointed out, there were always the grandparents, many of whom were survivors of concentration camps.

Although Vlasta would not meet my brother, who was living in Israel, until our reunion at Yad Vashem six years later, I rounded out the family picture with a few details of his life. I told her that a little over two years after our arrival in America her cousin, 'Toni Kašprišin', had enlisted in the United States Air Force and that a few months later, to his and our great amazement, he was selected 'Airman of the Month'. We both thought it was a truly American phenomenon that a young man coming from the country of *The Good Soldier Schweik* could be chosen for such an honour in so short a time. At the end of his military service, the GI Bill allowed him to convert his youthful love of tinkering, which we both remembered, into an engineering degree. If the America we found was not the land where the streets are paved with gold, it was surely the land of many possibilities. In telling our story, I was constantly aware of the contrast between the many opportunities which were given to us and the constrained circumstances under which Teta and Vlasta had to manage their lives.

Not surprisingly, Vlasta was most curious about my life – but I knew that we would have time during the rest of her stay to fill out the details. I told her about my six-year stint as a secretary, my undergraduate education in night school and my graduate training in philosophy. It was not easy to explain to her, late at night and in halting Slovak, my deep interest in moral philosophy, professional ethics and public policy which, I believe, have their roots in the chaotic world in which we both grew up. I was convinced that these interests have so strongly shaped the person I have become that, even if I could not explain myself clearly, she would understand the substance of what I tried to convey during her two-week stay with us.

As the sun rose in the morning, my stories were told and most of the gifts she brought had found their proper recipients. Some presents were left unassigned. She would hold on to them until she had had a chance to form her own impressions. By the end of her visit everything she brought was given away, sometimes in unexpected ways. Sleep did not come the first night. My body was ill and Vlasta was totally exhausted after two sleepless nights, but our spirits were high.

Vlasta's two-week stay was memorable for us and for her. We showed her New York, Philadelphia, Washington, D.C. and Baltimore, where we celebrated the New Year with old friends who put great stock in gourmet food and vintage wines – light years removed from our meagre war-time fare or from Vlasta's life in Slovakia. We lit a candle for Teta in Saint Patrick's Cathedral, an act both of us recalled vividly six years later when we stood in front of the Eternal Flame in the Tent of Remembrance in Yad Vashem. We went to the wedding of a very orthodox cousin in Brooklyn, where Vlasta was treated with great honour and reverence, and we attended a holiday performance of the Nutcracker Suite ballet in Princeton. We spent a day with my sister and her husband in Northern New Jersey, and Christmas morning walking in brisk sunshine through the nearly deserted streets of New Hope, Pennsylvania. Vlasta went to Mass with our neighbours across the street with whom we all shared dessert on Christmas day. Above all, we spent countless hours together talking, walking, cooking and reminiscing. I told her of my plan to write a book, dedicated to Teta, about the 'good people' we encountered during the war – those who saved our lives, and those who showed us unexpected kindness and generosity. In a sort of re-enactment of our childhood dreams of having full stomachs and wings to fly, I confessed my fantasy that the book would be an enormous success, that she and Teta would become famous, and that she could live comfortably on the royalties forever after. I did not include a movie contract!

When we were not travelling or visiting, we were shopping for things we wanted her to take back. These expeditions were agonizing for me, always a reluctant shopper. As a newcomer to our consumers' paradise, Vlasta was overwhelmed by the choices of products and the range of prices, and would spend hours picking out a small transistor radio, a solar calculator or an item of clothing. She could not understand my cavalier attitude toward shopping any more than I could comprehend her fear of making a mistake. The more I encouraged her to buy, the more time she took over each item. Standing in the aisles of large department stores and small boutiques, with aching feet and considerable impatience, I recalled the story that a Russian-born friend, Vlada Tolley, told me about her mother, a life-long denizen of Moscow. On her visits to America, Vlada's mother found herself totally disoriented and disheartened when shopping in a supermarket. Her anxiety was particularly pronounced when she passed the yoghurt counter. She saw the many varieties of brands, flavours, sizes, textures and prices not as consumer choices, but as the work of the devil trying to deceive her and trick her into buying the wrong thing. But Vlasta and I persevered, and on the day before her departure her suitcases were once again filled, this time with presents from us to her, and a few souvenirs she wanted to take back to her friends and co-workers. On the night before her departure we were pleased to discover that she needed an additional suitcase to fit in all the things we bought as well as presents given to her by my sister and friends. She would not allow us to pay for the things she bought for others, and we agreed that that was fair.

The two weeks of her visit passed quickly, and it was hard to say goodbye. During our final embrace at the airport, partly to ease the tension and partly because I wanted to put into words something I knew would be hard for me to do, I promised that, before too long, we would come to Košice to visit her. Although she understood how difficult the return journey would be for me, she said she was confident that I would act on my resolve and that my promise was the most precious thing she was taking back with her.

Just as well that promises cannot be stolen. When she picked up her suitcases at the airport in Slovakia she discovered, to her great sorrow, that most of the items we so carefully selected, collected and packed had been stolen somewhere between New York and Bratislava. Only the things in her carry-on case were untouched. It was probably not uncommon for luggage handlers on international flights from the United States to eastern Europe to break the locks of suitcases and pilfer their contents. Even had we been forewarned, there were not many precautions we could have taken, but we might have tried something. Now it was too late. We mourned the loss of material goods, but we kept alive the memories of her visit, and my promise to return to Slovakia. The promise was safe, and was fulfilled a year-and-a-half later when, in the summer of 1993, my husband and I travelled to Košice.

Vlasta's visit helped to fill the void between my childhood and my adult life, providing a connecting link between the person I had become and the adolescent girl who left Czechoslovakia in 1948. Her presence brought a reality and texture to the war years and gave my husband, daughter, and those of my friends she met, a deeper understanding of my formative years and of the effect they may have had on my temperament and my worldview. But she was loved and honoured not for building bridges, but for the person she was, as a child and as a mature woman, and for the memory of her mother that she brought with her.

10 Return

In a Slovak folk tale, an old peasant dies and is condemned to hell. Upon hearing his fate, he begs the keeper of the heavenly gates to show mercy and change the edict. Saint Peter hesitates, but in the end relents on condition that the peasant, who had lived a mean and selfish life, can provide evidence of a single good deed he had done in the course of his long life. This is a hard assignment, but with his eternal life at stake, the peasant finally remembers that once, in his youth, he gave a starving man an onion. Although Saint Peter is not impressed by the peasant's generosity, he agrees to suspend an onion from heaven. If the peasant, corpulent even in death, can pull himself up by its tail, he will be allowed to pass through the heavenly gates. In the final summation, the smallest act of charity counts and does not go unrewarded. Even an onion is a coin in the celestial realm. (This folk tale must have several variations, since a strikingly similar story is told by Grushenka in *The Brothers Karamazov*.)

My reluctance to visit Slovakia was deep and long standing. With overwhelmingly bleak and sad memories, I had neither the desire to reconnect with the land of my past, nor the curiosity to find out about conditions in the present. From time to time I had made half-hearted inquiries about obtaining a visa but I never followed through. What held me back was the recollection of the acute discomfort I had felt, on a summer day in the early 1960s, when my husband and I drove through Germany on our way from Holland to Denmark. As soon as we crossed the German border I went into psychological deep freeze. Although at that time I was still fluent in German, I did not seem to be able to engage in even the simplest transaction with the hotel clerk. I could speak German in Zurich and in Berne, but not in a provincial town in Germany. In the evening, I refused to leave our room to go out to dinner or take a stroll in the city. The sound of the language, the presence of so many Mercedes Benzes (the favoured car of SS officers) and even the echoes of footsteps on the pavements made me feel claustrophobic. I recognized that my reactions were excessive, and had we stayed a few days longer, I would probably have come out of my shell. But I had no desire to test my psychological resilience; all I wanted to do was to get out as fast as possible. I breathed a sigh of relief when we crossed the German-Danish border, as if we had closed the 'gates of hell' behind us. While I did not feel self-righteous about my response, neither did I struggle against it.

Much has changed in Germany since 1962. During the first two and a half post-war decades, for reasons that were in part economic and political and in part psychological, there was a 'conspiracy of silence' between the generation that lived through the war and, in one way or another, participated in it, and the generation that was born after the war. (In fairness, one must acknowledge that silence also prevailed between the survivors of the Holocaust and their children, who were either too young to understand the horror they had lived through, or who were born after the liberation.) The Holocaust was neither a subject of scholarly research nor of conversation. There seemed to be more urgent tasks — to rebuild a country and to rebuild individual lives. Beginning with the general ferment of the generation of the late 1960s, both in America and in Europe, the twelve years of Nazi rule entered centre stage. At the same time that German scholars, artists and activists focused on the shameful past with ever increasing specificity, Germany began to move gradually toward fully fledged membership in the European Community of Nations. With the reopening of the Reichstag in April 1999, the 'Berlin Republic' has, both historically and symbolically, grounded itself in the past, while looking toward the future. On a more personal level, knowledge of the past has allowed the younger generation to forge its own identity and to accept responsibility for the crimes committed in the name of the German *Volk*, without being burdened by guilt. Today, young Germans learn about the Holocaust, its perpetrators and its victims, from many different sources. Starting with the primary school curriculum all through the university years, they study the history of the Nazi era, its roots and its consequences. Outside the classroom the past is ever present. They read about it in the popular press and in the many books, some scholarly, others more general, some accusatory, a few revisionist, that are written in German or translated from other languages; they hear about it on television, in movies and in the theatre; and they see it in the many memorials and 'Houses of Memories' that are scattered throughout Germany. There is some concern, both inside and outside of Germany, that such intense focus on the past may lead to an obsession with it, or a trivialization of it, or perhaps both.

In the intervening years, I too have become wiser. I have learned, both on an intellectual and on an emotional level, that I cannot use the single lens of the Holocaust to judge contemporary Germany. By not cutting myself off from the works of present day German historians and artists I began to understand the efforts of the younger generation, particularly those who came to adulthood after the war, to accept the historical, moral and psychological burden imposed on them by the acts of their fathers and mothers, and their own commitment to building a just and democratic society. They seemed willing to take responsibility for events in which they had not participated, to confront their recent history and to live with knowledge of it without becoming paralyzed by it. But it has taken years to bring their efforts to fruition, with bumps along the way, and the task is by no means finished. Perhaps one of the great strengths of democracy in Germany is the vigilance of most segments of society against the rise of neo-Nazi groups. But if the shadow of the Nazi past haunts many post-war Germans, it also exercises a demonic attraction for some of the young and dispossessed. In a very different way, I myself am still not free of the past. When, a couple of years ago, my husband proposed a short trip to Berlin, I declined. Somewhat surprised by my response, I nevertheless accepted it. Understanding does not bring forgiveness, and forgiveness does not bring forgetfulness.

In sharp contrast with the post-war history of West Germany, Czechoslovakia, under communist rule, had not been engaged in reconnecting its political and legal institutions with the democratic policies and values that had guided the founding of the Republic in 1918. Preoccupied with internal struggles and external oppression, Czechoslovakia was a closed society ruled by tanks and a totalitarian ideology, not by democratic ideals. Even if the country did not have openly anti-Semitic policies – as was the case during the Slánský trials in the early 1950s – not much else seemed to have changed since the days we left Košice in 1948 except, of course, the break-up of the country into two independent republics on 1 January 1993. I thought of the Slovak region as fervently nationalistic and xenophobic and I feared that on my return I would be overwhelmed by echoes of the past.

Had I not promised Vlasta that I would come back, I probably would never have made the journey. But in a sense she was the 'onion' of the Slovak nation. After all, it was in recognition of the power of good deeds, even in the face of overwhelming evil, that I had promised to return. I also believed that both Vlasta's presence, and the presence of my husband, who was genuinely looking forward to our first excursion into eastern Europe, would soften the harsh, painful and half-forgotten past. As I discovered in June 1993, I was half right and half wrong.

We carefully planned our two-week stay – eight nights in Slovakia and six in the Czech Republic. Reverting to one of my childhood habits, retained over the years, of eating the spinach before tasting the meat, I wanted to get through our trip to Slovakia and then enjoy our stay in Prague, a beautiful city without any memories. I would start out as a pilgrim and then become a tourist.

When we landed in Prague on our way to Košice, I felt neither joy nor dread nor any other emotion except for a mild curiosity. I was, however, surprised to see that the distinction between the Czechs and the Slovaks, which I had so firmly carried in my head, probably with scant justification, as a moral divide, had become a political reality. The former Czechoslovakia now consisted of two independent countries, the Czech Republic and Slovakia, each with its own currency, customs and political institutions. I used the three-hour layover at the airport to change money, buy a soft drink and test my ability to communicate in Slovak. (Although Czech and Slovak are different languages, they are sufficiently similar for a Czech and a Slovak speaker to communicate without much difficulty. This is not the case with any other two Slavic languages.) My efforts were greeted with some surprise by the airport personnel. Although my pronunciation was nearly accentless, my grammar was abominable and my vocabulary pathetically poor. I spoke rapidly, using whatever words I could find rather than struggle to unearth the appropriate ones. Who was this person who spoke the language in such a strange way? I myself had difficulty identifying with the speaker. My voice did not seem to belong to me. The words appeared to come from some deep recesses of my being, as if I was a ventriloquist. I was glad we had a few hours at the airport – a sort of dress rehearsal for my return.

When we boarded our flight to Košice I became very apprehensive. Had I had the option of turning around and going back to New York, I may have done so. That not being possible, I thought of Teta and concentrated on seeing Vlasta again. A group of young, enthusiastic, singing missionaries, on their way from America to Russia, provided some distraction. Their songs in praise of the Lord mingled in my mind with the patriotic and sentimental songs sung by the Russian soldiers when they marched into Slovakia at the end of the war, and, alas, also with the hate-filled songs of the Hlinka Guard. It was my first intimation of how much the past and the present would become intertwined throughout our journey. Even singing had lost its innocence, and the line between the Lord and the Avenger was blurred.

With flowers in hand and a smile on her face, Vlasta waited for us at the airport. She was visibly excited to see us and perhaps somewhat surprised that the promise, made a year and a half before, had finally become a reality. We chatted non-stop all the way to the hotel, once again in the mixture of Slovak, English and Russian which we resorted to when my husband was present.

Throughout our stay, I was torn by conflicting thoughts and emotions. I knew how important it was for Vlasta that the visit go well and how eager she was to show me the places of our youth, the Jewish sites in the towns we visited, and the changes that have occurred in Slovakia since the fall of the communist regime. With great pride she pointed to the small shops, no more than holes in the walls, with meagre merchandise that she took to be the first modest manifestations of what could become a flourishing capitalist economy. She believed, and wanted to convince me, that things were different now from what they had been in the Slovakia I remembered and from the Slovakia in which she had lived most of her adult life. I could not in good conscience express doubts about a future for which she so fervently hoped and which might change her life.

Whatever my view of the future, I was a prisoner to the past. While I could seldom reconstruct specific events, I was flooded with feelings brought about by smells, signs and sounds around me. Everything seemed familiar, sinister and menacing. Walking home at night, I was apprehensive if there were footsteps behind us. When we visited Bardejovské Kúpele, a spa near the Polish border about an hour and a half by bus from Košice, where my family used to take the 'water cure', the mineral waters brought back not only the vile taste of rotten eggs that I used to hate, but also memories of the time my father told us that we could no longer go there. Spas had become off limits to Jews. Although I did not need the 'cure' and did not miss the mineral water, I sensed the larger significance of the exclusion from what used to be a carefree vacation spot. In the town of Bardejov, while my husband and Vlasta went sight seeing, I sat on a bench, surrounded by many churches with crosses and one dilapidated and no longer used synagogue. I could not be a tourist. Everywhere I went I was haunted by the past, covered up but not buried.

The crisis occurred on the day when Vlasta, with a great deal of thought and effort, had arranged for an excursion to the Tatra mountains. A friend with a car had volunteered to be our guide and our itinerary had been carefully planned. Intending to make an early start, we set the alarm to be sure we would awake on time. Long before the alarm went off, I woke up feeling sick and dizzy. When I tried to get out of bed, I could just as well have been riding a Ferris Wheel. Everything, including my head and stomach, was in motion. Whether the cause of my illness was bacterial, viral or psychological, did not matter at that moment; what did matter was that I was unable to get dressed and leave the room. Vlasta and my husband were disappointed, and much as I urged them to go without me, they refused. Instead they explored Košice, returning to the hotel from time to time to see how I was doing. I felt helpless and doubly guilty. Guilty for being less than generous to Vlasta, and guilty for spoiling the trip.

For me, the most peaceful moments of the trip were spent in Vlasta's apartment on the outskirts of Košice. The food she served, the photographs on the mantelpiece, the furniture, and even the small knick-knacks, brought back memories of Teta and of our lives before and shortly after the war. Only the television set, the telephone, the hair dryer and an assortment of electronic gadgets, many of them purchased in the United States and packed in her carry-on case, testified to the passage of time.

The three of us experienced things on different planes. Vlasta wanted to shed a gentler light on my Slovakia; my husband saw the country through the eyes of an engaged and curious tourist, with keen appreciation for architecture, landscape, and what can loosely be described as 'Slavic' culture. I was neither a native nor a tourist. I felt trapped and claustrophobic, yet no longer regretting my decision to come.

Vlasta was indefatigable. We explored Košice – both the familiar and the unfamiliar parts. We visited the apartment on Tajovského ulica no. 11 where we lived after the war. Walking through the rooms and hallways I had a dim recollection of having been there, but without any concrete recall of how the spaces had been configured and furnished, or what it had felt like to occupy them. Perhaps I would have remembered more if the apartment had not been converted to institutional use, if there had been clearly designated rooms with specific household functions, including a kitchen and a bathroom, but I am not sure. If it takes an effort to remember, I did not seem capable of making it.

We also stopped at the Girls' Gymnasium, which I had attended for three years. Walking through the building, guided by a custodian who seemed pleased by our interest, I experienced, rather than recalled, the past. The small classrooms, the blackboards, the coloured chalk, the drawings on the walls, seemed familiar and teased my memory, but produced only distant echoes. If I had hoped that Eva and Nuša, my classmates whose photographs I treasure, would emerge from one of the corridors and greet me, that did not happen. The school, which had recently celebrated its 40th anniversary, is now coeducational and has 800 students, of whom 180 had earned their *matura* or graduation certificate in the previous school year. It was spotlessly clean and well maintained, with 12 of its 30 classrooms equipped with computers and interactive videos. If only one could equate technological advances with moral progress.

In the late afternoons we walked on the '*Corso*', the main street of the town, where little seemed to have changed from the way I remembered it. Young women, dressed in their finery, walked arm in arm, and young men ogled them. Frequently a whole family was out for a stroll, with children running in front and parents bringing up the rear. We rested on park benches from which we had a fine view of the impressive Opera House, where, over 40 years ago, I had heard my first opera, *Madame Butterfly*, probably sung in Slovak. We watched the birds and listened to the town band playing classical and popular music. On the way to our hotel we passed by the Children's Hospital where the father of my only surviving childhood friend, another Eva, worked after the war until he and his family left for Israel in 1949, about the same time my father did. I also took several long walks by myself, deliberately getting lost in the hope of stirring memories, but to no avail. Most of them remained under lock and key. All our excursions were diversions from our main purpose – to visit the sites of Jewish communal life.

The life of the Jewish community of Košice, numbering about 300 people in 1993, most of whom are elderly survivors of concentration camps, is centred around the smaller of the two remaining synagogues, on Zvonárska ulica, and its adjacent community centre, which serves about 50 kosher meals a day, mostly to townspeople and the occasional tourist. The community also maintains a *mikvah* and a Hebrew school. When we visited the centre, Vlasta seemed more at ease than I was. She asked questions about the rabbi, the little school (only four children in attendance) and the restoration projects of the two main synagogues. The façade of the older synagogue was dilapidated, but both had beautiful, if neglected, interiors. The one on Zvonarská ulica is open daily, but the larger one on Puškinova ulica is used only on the High Holidays. Just as it happened when we toured the Gymnasium, I heard distant echoes of events that refused to surface with any clarity. I knew that I had been in the courtyard before, that I had spent some time playing in the shadows of the buildings, and that, at least during the High Holidays, I sat with my mother and sister in the women's section of the synagogue. But this knowledge was not accompanied by images or by emotions. I did not recapture memories, nor did I have a strong desire to store up the experiences of the present and share them with my mother and siblings when we got home. Neither in Košice, nor later in Prešov, with one exception, did I make any effort to find out whether people we had known were still living there. I wish I had had the generosity, if not the curiosity, to probe more deeply, but I did not. Just as after the war we felt guilty, and in a way ashamed, about our survival, I now felt reluctant to meet people who had suffered so much, and to whom my life would appear, and rightly so, full of opportunities and privileges. Once again I belonged to the lucky ones. My very tenuous link with the Jewish community in Košice is now an annual exchange of New Year's greetings with Pani Lauferová, the middle-aged woman who showed us around the courtyard and seemed well versed in the intricate affairs of communal life. She told us about the trials and tribulations of the newly arrived rabbi, an Australian who had come via Helsinki, and who was making efforts to introduce new, more modern ideas. These seem to have involved more integration of the Jewish community into the ongoing life of the city. Regarded with considerable scepticism by Pani Lauferová herself, they subsequently proved unsuccessful.

Our two trips to Prešov were also difficult. Except for the absence of its once thriving Jewish community, Prešov did not seem to have changed much since the time we lived there. It remains a small, pleasant and very clean provincial town, with well-paved tree-lined streets, lovely squares, many churches and handsome architecture. Our first visit to the synagogue, on a Saturday afternoon, was disappointing. Its windows appeared boarded up, its gates closed, with no sign of life either on the inside, or on the outside. While the mute presence of a building which I had associated with a flourishing Jewish life confirmed for me what I had expected, Vlasta responded with great indignation, as she did so often during our searches for traces of Jewish life in Slovakia. When she asked people on the street to show us the way to a synagogue or a monument and they told us that they did not know, she chastised them. 'You should know', was one of her constant refrains. The subtext was clear and urgent: 'You have no right to forget the Jews and what you did to them; you destroyed their lives and you cannot bring them back, but you must honour their memory.' Several days later, on our second trip to Prešov, we discovered that although the synagogue looked totally dilapidated on the outside (it was beautifully renovated and rededicated in August 1998), it was magnificent and well preserved on the inside. The community, once numbering 6,000, had 52 registered Jews. Services are held on Friday nights and on High Holidays, but not on Saturdays. Since we arrived in the middle of the day, during the synagogue's office hours, we had the good fortune of meeting the head of the community, Mr. Desire Landa, who became our guide. He remembered my father and he showed me the book about the history of the Jews of Prešov, which my father had written in 1940. Mr. Landa has himself written several historical and commemorative pieces about the Jewish community of Prešov, as well as an account of his survival in Auschwitz. Once again there were stirrings of memories, but nothing that I could get hold of and build upon. When I stood in the women's section of the synagogue I imagined that I heard the whispers and laughter of my mother and her friends, or perhaps even the voice of Moishe Paiser's young daughter or that of Vali Schwartz, my brother's first love, whose family had lived in one of the houses in the courtyard. But can ghosts speak, or can silence whisper? Was it memory, or was it imagination, and did it really matter? I tried to get in touch with one family friend who remained in Prešov and who I was told had left the courtyard shortly before we came, but after two unsuccessful telephone attempts I gave up. Again, it was an act of cowardice. Even if I had not ultimately succeeded, I should have tried harder.

Mr. Landa gave us precise directions to the apartment house on Kováčcka ulica where we had lived before the war. Alas, the building no longer existed. The ground on which it once stood has been converted to a parking lot. I wondered briefly whether there was some sort of justice in the physical disappearance of a home from which we had been evicted. But I also tried hard to imagine the configuration of our apartment, to remember the view we had of the Bašta, a tower like fortification which we could see from our windows, and to evoke some memories of our lives there. But like the house itself, the memories no longer exist. The parking lot had nothing to do with my childhood.

On our second visit to Prešov we took a stroll on the Tabor, a hilly section of town, where my paternal grandparents had lived for many years before the war. I remembered my mother taking my brother and me to the Tabor to cure our whooping cough. It had the best and cleanest mountain air available to us! I also remembered the walnut trees in the garden, although they had disappeared, probably to make room for expanding the house. As children, we were not allowed to shake the trees to coax them into yielding their nuts. Instead we had to wait until they fell on the ground, a sign that they were ripe enough to crack and eat. But it was a catch twenty-two situation. My paternal grandmother, always exceedingly frugal, would gather the walnuts as soon as they fell off the trees and store them for later use. The Tabor was the only place that brought back pleasant memories. My grandfather died before the war; my grandmother perished in a concentration camp in the summer of 1944.

We had one encounter in Prešov which fairness dictates that I recount. To my husband's great distress (he is an avid photographer, especially of landscapes and buildings), the knob that turned the film on our camera came off. After several unsuccessful efforts to refasten it, we stopped by a small photography shop in one of the squares. A young man, with a welcoming smile and great eagerness to help, repaired it in no time. He was so young, so kind, so concerned that we be able to record our trip, that for a brief moment I felt free and happy. Maybe he is representative of the new generation. Maybe out of the past, as it remains entombed in my mind, can come a promising future.

The most painful part of our trip was yet to come – it happened during our visit to the town of Nitra. We set out early in the morning, in a half-empty bus with two bus drivers. The 180-mile-long trip took seven and a half hours to complete, with several stops in run down and mostly deserted bus stations. Vlasta and I whiled away the time reminiscing. Her memory of our lives together was much sharper than mine, and while she talked, I took notes furiously. I needed the fragments for the story I wanted to write.

Our arrival in Nitra, on a dark, stormy and rainy evening, was inauspicious. The streets were empty and there were no taxicabs in sight. In no time our drenched bodies were in tune with our sagging spirits. After some moments of indecision, we took public transportation to our hotel, and quickly settled in. Dinner at the hotel was restful and for Vlasta, who seldom had the luxury of eating out, it was a special treat. As soon as the rain stopped we went for a walk. We wandered through the deserted centre of town and then headed for Palánok, the section of town where we lived with my mother's uncle and his family for a few months in the summer of 1944, just before we went into hiding. I was glad that our building, Number 5, no longer existed. All that was left was a pile of rubble on an empty lot. I remembered nothing about the house, or our apartment. I felt intense pain as I recalled how my Uncle David, my Aunt Ida and their son Immy had been caught hiding in the attic in the last year of the war. I thought of Immy and his harmonica and I imagined that I heard his music – a brief, haunting reprieve in an otherwise stark tableau.

Up to this point my sleep in Slovakia had been dreamless, or at least, if that is not possible, I did not recall any dreams when I woke up in the morning. During the first night in Nitra I had a dream so vivid and so colourful that, upon awakening, I needed some time to reorient myself to the present. I wish I remembered the language in which the events of the dream took place, but I do not. Slovak? German? English? In the dream I was invited by a woman from Sarah Lawrence College, where I had my first teaching job, to give a lecture on the topic: How can one teach moral precepts to young people who live in an immoral world? When my husband and I arrived at the appointed place and time, the hall, which resembled the dining room in the Jewish community centre in Košice, was filled to capacity. One table was reserved for vegetarians. (I have since tried, unsuccessfully, to decipher the meaning of the 'vegetarian' option. Did it stand for those who were different from others, perhaps on a higher moral plane, perhaps more connected with the natural order? Or was it simply a metaphor for kosher food?)

The presence in the dining room of so many people wanting to hear me on a topic about which, I suddenly realized, I understood nothing, filled me with panic. Do I run? Do I pretend to know something when, in fact, I do not know anything? Do I confess ignorance and ask the audience for help? I know that I stayed and delivered the talk. Fortunately, or unfortunately, I do not remember much of its substance or its point. I have a vague recollection of trying to use metaphors for the absence of absolute moral standards to emphasize that, however we come

124

to terms with a failed or hidden God, we have to create expectations based on our capacities as ordinary human beings and on the reality of the moral vocabulary by which we judge our deeds and the deeds of others. I did not wake up with applause ringing in my ears – but neither did I wake up in a cold sweat. I assume that, if I accomplished nothing else in the dream, I at least started a discussion about the place and grounding of morality in a secular world. Whatever nightmare quality the dream had, it came not from what others were doing to me, but from my own ignorance. In some ways, the dream may be connected with a question I have asked myself often over the years, and which came back to me with full force during our visit – how would I have acted had I been an ordinary citizen of Slovakia? It has always been easy to dismiss the possibility of active collaboration; it has been more difficult to dismiss the possibility of remaining an uninvolved and therefore complicit bystander. It has been, and remains to this day, impossible to claim that I would have become a rescuer. Perhaps I was judging others by standards that were harsher than the ones that, in similar circumstances, I would have accepted for myself.

The next day we set out early, in bright sunshine. What made our exploration of Nitra different from our visits to other cities was that here, Vlasta and I shared many experiences. We both arrived in Nitra in the summer of 1944, and our lives were intertwined for over a year.

Etched in our memories were not only places and events, but also feelings of loss and terror. We walked mostly in silence. Our first stop was again on Palánok and the nearby large, well-preserved but unused synagogue on Pri Synagóge ulica. The Jews are gone, the synagogue is no longer in use, but the name of the street has remained unchanged. We walked on the banks of the river Nitra and I remembered that, in September of 1944, on the second day of Rosh Hashanah, my family and the other remaining Jews of Nitra went for *tashlich*, when it is customary to drop crumbs into flowing water to symbolize, at least according to one interpretation, the washing away of sins. Did we have sins for which we had not yet been punished? And had our sins not been washed away, would we have been saved?

Our trip to the Čráň brought back many memories for both Vlasta and me. After all these years, neither of us remembered how to get there, and we had to ask several people for directions – first to the section of the Čráň, and then to Čulenova ulica where we had lived. Although the sun was warm and comforting, I remembered the long, cold, winter afternoons when my brother and I trudged across the bridge to get wood and coal from the forest and the railroad tracks on the other side of town, and then climbed the steep streets to get back home. We walked to save money, and to avoid being trapped in a routine inspection conducted randomly on a tramcar or a bus. As long as we were in an open space we could always run and hide – or so we thought. When we arrived at our destination it was vastly different from what either of us had remembered. The small, one room workers' cottages, with a kitchen, a pantry, a narrow hallway, an attic and an outhouse, had been replaced by much more substantial, small, but well-kept family homes with flower gardens and indoor plumbing. Would it have been more comforting to find the place unchanged? I don't think so. At least in some ways I was relieved that the house on Palánok had become a pile of rubble, that the cottages on Čulenova ulica had been transformed, that the synagogue at the heart of what once was the Jewish section was no longer in use. The Nitra of my childhood no longer existed.

We spent the rest of the afternoon wandering around – Vlasta and I as 'accidental tourists', without much curiosity or enthusiasm. Only my husband enjoyed the exploration of the city – the long walk to the Castle, the view of the new Arts Centre, and the hustle of the late afternoon shopping crowds. If I needed confirmation of my dim view of the city, it was provided by a middle aged Slovak nationalist whom we encountered on the Plaza in front of the Arts Centre who, with genuine hospitality, offered to show us around. In the course of our conversation (actually, more of a monologue), he told us that he mistrusted the Czechs because they were always scheming to dominate the Slovaks; he was leery of the Hungarians, because they cheat; he disliked the Gypsies, because they steal; and he hated the Russians, because they had suppressed the aspirations of the Slovak nation. He dreamt that now that Slovakia was rid of the Czechs and the Russians, the government would deal decisively with the Hungarians and the Gypsies, and then the Slovak people would show the world the great things they could accomplish. His nationalistic and xenophobic rhetoric, his sense of victimization and his aggressive bravado, reminded me of the language of the Hlinka Guard. I did not inquire about his views of Jews. There were too few of them left to make a difference, but anti-Semitism can flourish even without the physical presence of Jews.

We arrived back at the hotel just before another torrential rainstorm, accompanied by thunder and lightning, broke over the city. It was comforting to be inside, sheltered both from memories and from the elements.

Our stay was coming to an end, and our last dinner together was strained. I felt sad about parting from Vlasta and relieved that I was leaving, probably never to come back. Vlasta was devastated by our imminent departure. My husband would have cheerfully spent a few more days in Slovakia. We knew how each one of us felt, and we acknowledged the inevitability of the differences among us, but we did not want to talk about them.

The following morning we set out by bus for Bratislava, the capital of Slovakia, about an hour and a half away. The city held no memories for me, so it was easy just to stroll around the banks of the Danube, sit in a cafe and, at Vlasta's insistence, visit the sites of several synagogues. For the last time she had a chance to berate a cabdriver who did not know where the main synagogue was, as if he was ignorant about the existence of an important national monument. We knew that we had run out of time to say important things to each other, so we settled for chitchat and a dish of ice cream in a local outdoor cafe.

Vlasta came with us to the airport and waited for our plane to depart for Prague before heading back to the city to embark on the long train ride to Košice. This time, our suitcases were filled with presents she bought for us, and for each member of our family, as well as for the friends she had made on her visit to the States. There was no easy way to say goodbye, so I whispered the phrase from the Passover service: 'Next year in Jerusalem'. It was at that moment, I believe, that I saw with absolute clarity that both Vlasta and Teta deserved to be inscribed in Yad Vashem and that our next reunion should take place in Israel. It took four years for it to happen, but we now had a goal we wanted to achieve – one that would unite the spirit of Teta, Vlasta and members of the family they saved in one place.

Always circums-
pection!

& yet
unconnected
unmoved
&
yet moved

Good Beyond Evil

Over the years, I have reflected on my trip to Slovakia. Was I too harsh and unforgiving in my judgements? Did I filter out the good and concentrate only on the bad? Did I feel duty bound not to like anything, not to forgive anything? In casual encounters we did meet a number of young people who were eager to get on with building their lives, who yearned for a free society and for a chance to travel and explore. On the other hand, many of the old ways, and old hatreds, seemed securely in place. There is once again a Hlinka Street in Košice – at the time of our visit, still relegated to the outskirts of the town. When I asked Vlasta about it she said, with considerable bitterness, that it might not be long before Hlinka, or even Father Tiso, would have the main streets of Košice named for them. The letter I wrote to my family upon our return ended on the following note:

I found the trip difficult, mostly because there were no good memories, or old friends, or familiar places, that would have connected positively with the past. In many ways I found Slovakia unchanged. Everybody seems to be glad that the days of communism are over, but in Slovakia it appears to have been replaced by a great deal of nationalism, xenophobia, sense of victimization and a certain amount of bravado. There are signs of individual initiative and a desire for change, and Vlasta proudly pointed out all the places which are now operated by small entrepreneurs, rather than by state collectives. The country is clean, shabby and turned in on itself. The stores are relatively empty and it is not uncommon to go into a very large space and find very few items for sale. Food is plentiful and, at least in the summer, fruit and vegetables are abundant. Durable goods appear to be imported and way beyond the means of ordinary people. Objectively, Slovakia has soft borders, large and at times troublesome minorities (Gypsies, Hungarians, Ukrainians, Romanians) and it is saddled with a heavy, industrial infrastructure that is not nimble enough to operate in the modern world. We encountered some really nice people, especially among the younger ones, who seemed hard working, optimistic and forward looking. But on the whole (and especially in

128

contrast to the Czech republic), Slovakia seemed caught in the time warp of 1945.

Were I to write this letter today, I would undoubtedly present a different, sunnier view of the material conditions of Slovakia. I wonder what I would have to say about the people – their everyday lives, their thoughts, their values, their fears and their hatreds. Whatever the facts may be, I somehow do not think that even today I would experience the 'return' in a gentler way. Yet I must not forget the nice young people. They are the hope of the future. For me, Slovakia is the place where we survived the war and where Teta and Vlasta have lived all their lives. It is a place I tried to forget, but having returned for a visit I now know that I neither can, nor want to, expunge it from my memory.

- Does one remember or not?
- Is memory divided into recognition + feelings?
- perhaps other elements?

As if a dialog in a journal

Epilogue

Vlasta and I are both approaching old age. The world of our childhood no longer exists. Our memories are faded and selective.

The lives of Teta and Vlasta were narrowly circumscribed, while my family and I were given a new beginning. Over the years, our paths became increasingly divergent. We continued to shape our futures and reap the benefits of living in a free and democratic society, but their horizons remained bounded and their opportunities limited. And yet, they remain rich in righteousness and moral virtue, and we remain their debtors. One can never repay adequately the gift of life, or sufficiently celebrate the courage to oppose evil and stand at the side of the oppressed. And so, after one has acknowledged the debt, in public and in private, the question still remains – can one do more?

One can keep the memory alive. In one's own life one can cling to the possibility that good is stronger than evil; one can continue to nourish the ties of love, respect and caring; and one can continue to tell the story of those who believed in good beyond evil.

Postscript

On May 1998, a year after the ceremony at Yad Vashem, Vlasta was granted a life-long pension from the Jewish Foundation for the Righteous. The mission of the Foundation, supported by the American Jewish community, is 'to repay a debt of gratitude to people who rescued Jews and are recognized by Yad Vashem as "Righteous Among the Nations"'. The Foundation currently provides pensions to about 1,300 rescuers in 25 countries. A few of them live in Slovakia. Having occasionally been asked to translate the letters they write to the Foundation, I have come to appreciate the enormous difference these pensions make to the quality of their old age, materially and spiritually. They provide a measure of physical comfort and remind them that their lives continue to be celebrated and that their deeds have not been forgotten.

Chronological Table

1938 – 29 September: Munich Agreement. Northern part of Bohemia (Sudetenland) is ceded to Germany.

1939 – 14 March: Partition of Czechoslovakia. Slovakia becomes an independent republic headed by Father Jozef Tiso. (The Czech lands and Moravia become a German protectorate.)

1939 – Spring: Ruthenian and Subcarpathian regions in the easternmost part of Slovakia are annexed by Hungary. Slovakia expels the Jews who live along the newly created borders as well as all 'stateless' Jews.

1939 – Spring: Tiso establishes a Department of Jewish Affairs.

1939–41: Series of harsh anti-Jewish measures, designed to isolate the Jews, deprive them of their livelihood, and exclude them from the arts and professions. Jews are not allowed to attend public schools; own radios or telephones; live in apartments that front main streets; leave their homes after dark, etc.

1940 – August: Dieter Wisličeny, Adolph Eichmann's deputy, arrives in Slovakia to advise the Department of Jewish Affairs.

1940 – September: Government establishes *Ústredna Židov* (ÚŽ) in Bratislava. It is the only official Jewish institution allowed to represent the Jews to the government, transmit government edicts to the Jews and ensure compliance with them.

1941 – June: Slovakia officially enters the Second World War as an ally of Germany.

1941 – September: Promulgation of the Jewish Codex, exceeding in harshness the Nuremberg Laws (1933–35). Jews are defined as an undesirable race sharing common, genetically transmitted traits. All edicts against the Jews, developed over a period of two and a half years, are gathered in a single, legally binding, document.

1942 – February: My father becomes the head of a newly established branch of the ÚŽ in Prešov.

1942 – March/October: First large deportations of Jews from Slovakia. In the beginning, only able bodied young men and women who are not married are sent to labour camps; later whole families are deported, mostly to Auschwitz. By the end of October, roughly 75 per cent of the Jews of Slovakia have been deported.

1942 – December: My brother and I are sent to Hungary.

1942 – December to mid-February 1943: My brother and I live in orphanages in Košice (by then part of Hungary).

1943 – Mid-February to 1 April: My brother and I are interned in a camp in Ricse (Hungary).

1943 – 1 April to early April 1944: My brother and I live with our uncle and his family in Tolcsva (Hungary).

1943 – Summer: Second wave of deportations of Jews from Slovakia, lasting several weeks. Stopped after payment of ransom.

1944 – March: Germany occupies Hungary.

1944 – April: Hungarian Jews are herded into ghettos. My aunt, uncle, their children, my grandmother, another aunt and my brother and I are taken to the Sátoraljaújhely ghetto.

1944 – Spring: Slovak Government orders the deportation of all remaining Jews. My parents and sister hide in Teta's apartment. A few days later, the edict is changed and Jews in the eastern part of Slovakia (including Prešov) are ordered to move to places further west. My family is assigned to go to Nitra.

1944 – 13 May: My brother and I are rescued from the ghetto and return to Prešov.

1944 – 15 May: Our family, Teta and Vlasta leave for Nitra.

1944 – 18 May: Start of the deportation of Jews from the Sátoraljaújhely ghetto.

1944 – June or July: My brother and I are given false papers and go to live with Teta and Vlasta in a house they recently rented on the outskirts of Nitra. My parents and sister continue to live in the city of Nitra.

1944 – 29 August: Slovak partisan uprising in Banská Bystrica.

1944 – October: Partisans are defeated. Orders are issued for the deportation of all remaining Jews in Slovakia.

1944 – October to March 1945: My parents, sister and a cousin move in with Teta, Vlasta, my brother and me. They do not have false papers.

1945 – 31 March: Liberation.

1945 – late summer: We move to Košice (now in Czechoslovakia).

1948 – 2 November: My mother, siblings and I arrive in America.

1949 – Spring: My father moves to Israel.

1991 – Christmas: Reunion with Vlasta.

1993 – Summer: Visit to Slovakia.

1997 – 3 July: Ceremony at Yad Vashem.

1998 – May: Vlasta receives a lifetime pension from the Jewish Foundation for the Righteous.

☐ What memoirs of the Holocaust have you read

Questions

☐ The last ¶ in the epilogue is quite moving, as it answers the questions: "Can one do more?".

you suggest 3° things: The first is intriguing ¹) one can (cling) to the possibility that good is stronger than →

that makes a lot of sense

⑤ I wonder if you think it's possible that evil is stronger than good?

see p 44 — kadish w/ Vlasta

☐ Your project — which draws its focus on those who ~~stood~~ believed in good beyond evil ↓

☐ The Role of memory — esp. p 25 in t narr for those who experienced tradgedy. What is "a memory" is it a "static", changing thing? See p 122 See 118? p T 150 p8f t par

(Eva / Nusa)?

☐ Have you thought about the meaning of Job? Does "it" have any application to what happened in Europe in 1930's — 40's? Does it explain suffering? Does it disappe See the end of Job, especially

☐ Psalm of Lament

Recall dream yours,
bottom of 124

☐ What role does faith "play,
(did) your
in your your life is it
(A.F. now) Has it changed
over the years? How so?

☐ What do you think is meant
the by human nature";?
Specifically, p 83 Lost trust
in human decency?

☐ Story of piano-playing,
Russian officer & passover
what does passover mean
in the context of Holocaust?

Questions on Autobiog: ☐
① What role does truth play?
in fact-telling
② Does the narrating process
distort?
③ Are there sure ways to
tell truth?

Questions:
☐ Unanswered? p 37